Gambling

Other Books of Related Interest:

At Issue Series

Indian Gaming

"Congress shall make
no law ... abridging
the freedom of speech,
or of the press."

First Amendment to the U.S. Constitution

The basic foundation of our democracy is the First Amendment guarantee of freedom of expression. The Opposing Viewpoints Series is dedicated to the concept of this basic freedom and the idea that it is more important to practice it than to enshrine it.

Gambling

David Haugen and Susan Musser, Book Editors

GREENHAVEN PRESS

An imprint of Thomson Gale, a part of The Thomson Corporation

Detroit • New York • San Francisco • New Haven, Conn. • Waterville, Maine • London

THOMSON

*

™

GALE

Christine Nasso, *Publisher*
Elizabeth Des Chenes, *Managing Editor*

© 2007 Thomson Gale, a part of The Thomson Corporation.

Thomson and Star logo are trademarks and Gale and Greenhaven Press are registered
trademarks used herein under license.

For more information, contact:
Greenhaven Press
27500 Drake Rd.
Farmington Hills, MI 48331-3535
Or you can visit our Internet site at http://www.gale.com

LIBRARY OF CONGRESS CATALOGING-IN-PUBLICATION DATA

Gambling / David Haugen and Susan Musser, book editors.
    p. cm. -- (Opposing viewpoints)
    Includes bibliographical references and index.
    ISBN-13: 978-0-7377-3352-5 (hardcover)
    ISBN-13: 978-0-7377-3353-2 (pbk.)
    1. Gambling--United States. 2. Gambling--Social aspects--United States.
    3. Gambling--Research--United States. I. Haugen, David M., 1969- II. Musser,
Susan.
    HV6715.G284 2007
    363.4'20973--dc22

                                                                        2007002994

ISBN-10: 0-7377-3352-7 (hardcover)
ISBN-10: 0-7377-3353-5 (pbk.)

Printed in the United States of America
10 9 8 7 6 5 4 3 2 1

Contents

Chapter 3: Is Compulsive Gambling a Problem?

Chapter 4: How Are Lottery Innovations Affecting Society and the Gaming Industry?

Why Consider
Opposing Viewpoints?

> *"The only way in which a human being
> can make some approach to knowing the
> whole of a subject is by hearing what
> can be said about it by persons of every
> variety of opinion and studying all
> modes in which it can be looked at by
> every character of mind. No wise man
> ever acquired his wisdom in any mode
> but this."*
>
> *John Stuart Mill*

In our media-intensive culture it is not difficult to find differing opinions. Thousands of newspapers and magazines and dozens of radio and television talk shows resound with differing points of view. The difficulty lies in deciding which opinion to agree with and which "experts" seem the most credible. The more inundated we become with differing opinions and claims, the more essential it is to hone critical reading and thinking skills to evaluate these ideas. Opposing Viewpoints books address this problem directly by presenting stimulating debates that can be used to enhance and teach these skills. The varied opinions contained in each book examine many different aspects of a single issue. While examining these conveniently edited opposing views, readers can develop critical thinking skills such as the ability to compare and contrast authors' credibility, facts, argumentation styles, use of persuasive techniques, and other stylistic tools. In short, the Opposing Viewpoints series is an ideal way to attain the higher-level thinking and reading skills so essential in a culture of diverse and contradictory opinions.

In addition to providing a tool for critical thinking, Opposing Viewpoints books challenge readers to question their own strongly held opinions and assumptions. Most people form their opinions on the basis of upbringing, peer pressure, and personal, cultural, or professional bias. By reading carefully balanced opposing views, readers must directly confront new ideas as well as the opinions of those with whom they disagree. This is not to simplistically argue that everyone who reads opposing views will—or should—change his or her opinion. Instead, the series enhances readers' understanding of their own views by encouraging confrontation with opposing ideas. Careful examination of others' views can lead to the readers' understanding of the logical inconsistencies in their own opinions, perspective on why they hold an opinion, and the consideration of the possibility that their opinion requires further evaluation.

Evaluating Other Opinions

To ensure that this type of examination occurs, Opposing Viewpoints books present all types of opinions. Prominent spokespeople on different sides of each issue as well as well-known professionals from many disciplines challenge the reader. An additional goal of the series is to provide a forum for other, less known, or even unpopular viewpoints. The opinion of an ordinary person who has had to make the decision to cut off life support from a terminally ill relative, for example, may be just as valuable and provide just as much insight as a medical ethicist's professional opinion. The editors have two additional purposes in including these less-known views. One, the editors encourage readers to respect others' opinions—even when not enhanced by professional credibility. It is only by reading or listening to and objectively evaluating others' ideas that one can determine whether they are worthy of consideration. Two, the inclusion of such viewpoints encourages the important critical thinking skill of objectively evaluating an author's credentials and bias. This evaluation will illuminate an author's reasons for taking a particular stance on an issue and will aid in readers' evaluation of the author's ideas.

It is our hope that these books will give readers a deeper understanding of the issues debated and an appreciation of the complexity of even seemingly simple issues when good and honest people disagree. This awareness is particularly important in a democratic society such as ours in which people enter into public debate to determine the common good. Those with whom one disagrees should not be regarded as enemies but rather as people whose views deserve careful examination and may shed light on one's own.

Thomas Jefferson once said that "difference of opinion leads to inquiry, and inquiry to truth." Jefferson, a broadly educated man, argued that "if a nation expects to be ignorant and free . . . it expects what never was and never will be." As individuals and as a nation, it is imperative that we consider the opinions of others and examine them with skill and discernment. The Opposing Viewpoints series is intended to help readers achieve this goal.

David L. Bender and Bruno Leone,
Founders

Introduction

> *"Once one form of gambling has been legalized, the anti-gambling arguments based on morality begin to fade away. Legalization of gambling seems to correspond with a general trend toward permissiveness in society. The Victorian morality that says nothing is permitted is replaced by the belief that everything is permitted, so long as you do not hurt another person. And gambling is the least harmful of the victimless crimes."*
>
> —I. Nelson Rose,
> Gambling and Public Policy:
> International Perspectives

> *"Over the past 50 years, gambling has gone from sin to vice to guilty pleasure and has come, finally, to be simply another point of interest on the entertainment map."*
>
> —Jonathan V. Last,
> Wall Street Journal

In late August 2005 Hurricane Katrina devastated New Orleans, Louisiana, as flood waters swamped many of the city's homes and businesses, including the 115,000-square-foot Harrah's New Orleans casino along the Mississippi River. On the day after the hurricane's landfall, Gary Loveman, the chief executive officer of Harrah's casinos, appeared on CNN to project his thoughts on the city's recovery. "We hope to work with Gov. Barbour in Mississippi in particular to get at least temporary casinos open as quickly as possible and get everybody back to work," he said.

Though Loveman's comment may sound unusual given the emergency priorities that follow a disaster, the sentiment may not have been out of place. Harrah's New Orleans provides jobs to 2,500 residents. It also generated revenues in excess of $300 million in 2004 with over $62 million being paid to the state in taxes. This income is the result of the more than 6.5 million customers who visited the casino and its hotel complex in that year, ensuring that the relatively new venture remains the state's largest tourist attraction. Without question, Harrah's New Orleans is a significant part of the city's economic strength. That it has become such a vital element, however, is perhaps far more interesting because it reveals how accepted and entrenched gambling has become in American society.

Just as Harrah's New Orleans has become integral to that city, casino gambling nationwide has become a significant economic force. According to the American Gaming Association, commercial casinos employ roughly 354,000 people and help generate another 450,000 jobs in businesses that contract with casinos. Commercial casinos raked in $31.85 billion in 2005, with $4.9 billion of that being handed over to the governments of the eleven states that have legalized casino gambling. And commercial casinos are just one segment of the gambling industry in America. Card rooms, Native American casinos, bingo parlors, racetracks, and lotteries added another $52.8 billion to gaming revenues in 2005. State lotteries alone brought in $22.89 billion, making them the second most profitable enterprise behind commercial casinos, and, unlike their counterparts, lotteries exist in forty-two states and the District of Columbia.

The pervasiveness of gambling in America and its contributions to state treasuries goes hand in hand with its growing popularity. More than one-quarter of adult Americans visited a casino in 2005, and more than 57 percent of Americans purchased a lottery ticket. Such statistics are not surprising, given that a 2005 Gallup poll found that two-thirds of the country's population approves of gambling, while other surveys place the percentage of tolerance even higher. This is in stark contrast to national views five decades ago when more than half the public opposed legalized gambling. Today, Americans even patronize illegal gambling in record numbers. Christiansen Capital Advisors, an entertainment industry analysis and management firm, estimates that approximately 8 million U.S. citizens gambled on the Internet in 2005, even though the federal government maintains that wagering on the Web violates U.S. laws.

The growth of Internet wagering—which now has exceeded two thousand independent sites offering everything from slots to poker to sports betting—is just the latest form of gambling's expansion. For most of the twentieth century, legalized gambling in America was limited to the casino trade in Las Vegas, Nevada, and some horse-racing tracks operating mainly east of the Mississippi River. In 1964, however, the gambling landscape changed when New Hampshire inaugurated a state lottery, the first to reemerge after the inglorious collapse of lotteries in the late nineteenth century. Several states followed New Hampshire's lead when it became clear that the enterprise was popular and provided a boost to the state's income.

Then in 1978, New Jersey opened the door to casino gambling's expansion when Atlantic City's leadership convinced the local constituents that casinos could help restore the former glory of the community's dilapidated boardwalk area. Although the project suffered a rocky start, revenues steadily increased. The trend in capitalizing on gambling proceeds hit the Midwest in the late 1980s in the form of riverboat casinos. But these experiments in revenue-raising paled in comparison to the casino boom that took place on Indian lands around that time. In 1988 President Ronald Reagan approved the passage of the Indian Gaming Regulatory Act, a federal statute that acknowledged that neither the federal nor state governments had any right to stop America's native tribes from operating gaming ventures on Indian land. Within a few years, several states began signing agreements with tribes to help smooth the building and servicing of the casinos for a slice of the profits. The partnership proved extremely lucrative for both the tribes and the states. Finally, in the new millennium, many of America's racetracks joined the casino bandwagon and adopted casino-style gambling in order to keep flagging interest in horse racing from closing down these venerable entertainment outlets.

With the spread of casinos and lotteries, as well as other gaming outlets, gambling has become commonplace in twenty-first-century America. As Jonathan V. Last, the online editor of the *Weekly Standard*, contends, "Its sheer ubiquity has made wagering seem banal, a normal part of middle-class life—something that only a prude would object to." Last believes that the recent popularity of poker is an example of how a former casino game has become "domesticated" and thus evades any serious social condemnation.

The prudes, or even milder critics of gambling's commonplace status in America, however, warn that domesticating gambling may exacerbate social problems associated with it. Some detractors, for example, insist that brick-and-mortar casinos encourage those in the surrounding community to gamble more often, and some claim that casinos foster a host of civic problems from crime to traffic congestion. More pernicious to the majority of critics, however, is the rise of Internet gambling. Ease of access to gambling Web sites has many worried that underage gamblers may be encouraged to play and jeopardize their meager finances or perhaps their college tuition. Others fear that even adults left alone in front of a computer screen are more likely to wager and chase their losses because there is no one around to restrain them. Such isolated gambling behavior has convinced some critics that addiction will result, thus increasing the number of problem gamblers in the United States.

Gambling's defenders, conversely, maintain that the spread of gambling in America is simply a case of supply meeting demand. The industry thrives because most people find it an acceptable form of entertainment. In *Opposing Viewpoints: Gambling*, proponents of the industry champion the supposed economic contributions and simple excitement that gaming provides, while gambling's critics examine the potential—and in some cases actual—negative consequences of its expansion. These debates are explored in chapters that ask the questions: How Does Legalized Gambling Affect Society? How Should the U.S. Government Respond to Internet Gambling? Is Compulsive Gambling a Problem? How Are Lottery Innovations Affecting Society and the Gaming Industry? Together, the chapters in this volume delve into the controversies that have arisen at this time in American history when gambling has become pervasive and socially acceptable.

OPPOSING VIEWPOINTS® SERIES

CHAPTER 1

How Does Legalized Gambling Affect Society?

Chapter Preface

Gambling in the United States has its share of advocates and opponents. Numerous arguments have been given for and against its impact on society, but most often those who favor legalized gambling quickly refer to the economic benefits for state treasuries and local businesses, while those who prefer to end or at least curb gambling commonly raise moral objections or cite its purported social harms.

The American Gaming Association (AGA), a casino industry lobby, is one of the most vocal champions of most land-based forms of gaming. The AGA contends that casinos provide jobs and bring in much-needed tax money to struggling areas. They also provide—in the AGA's view—a base of customers that will often patronize nearby stores, restaurants, and other businesses, increasing revenues that the entire host community will share. Frank J. Fahrenkopf Jr., the president and chief spokesperson of the AGA, summed up the economic benefits of the gaming industry in September 2005 in a speech to the Congressional Black Caucus's Annual Legislative Conference: "The 445 casinos in 11 states generated nearly 29 billion dollars in gross revenues in 2004" while creating "350,000 direct jobs paying more than 12 billion dollars in salaries, including benefits." Raising the standard of living in casino communities, Fahrenkopf maintains, improves quality of life and thus contributes to the general betterment of these areas.

Critics of gambling, however, are not so awed by the economic statistics. Even though the revenues are high, casino opponents estimate that the social costs are also great. They insist that casinos invite crime, cause civic congestion, and draw in problem gamblers whose addiction demands costly social services. A 2003 study analyzed these latter societal costs and found that among southern Nevadans alone the price tag can range between $300 million to $450 million a year. These figures were derived from bankruptcy and court case costs related to gambling losses, as well as from the cost of treatment of problem gamblers and revenues lost when these individuals ceased working as a result of their gambling troubles.

As long as gambling remains a mainstay of American life, advocates on both sides of the debate will continue to argue the costs and benefits. In the following chapter expert commentators offer their arguments on the possible benefits and potential harms of legalized gambling in the United States.

> *"Gambling obviously provides a kind of recreational excitement for some, but the cost to individuals, families, the economy, and society is too high to justify it."*

Legalized Gambling Hurts Communities

For Faith & Family

For Faith & Family is a Southern Baptist broadcast ministry under the direction of Dr. Richard Land. The ministry began in 1998 and is now carried by more than six hundred broadcast and Internet radio stations. In the following viewpoint, the ministry argues that legalized gambling harms communities by breeding crime, encouraging immoral behaviors, and negatively affecting the lives of gamblers and their families. In addition, For Faith & Family maintains that the supposed economic benefits of gambling are paltry and do not compensate for the devastation caused by this harmful vice.

As you read, consider the following questions:

1. How does legalized gambling promote community corruption, according to For Faith & Family?

2. In the author's view, how does gambling destroy innocent lives?

3. For Faith & Family contends that a successful plan to end the gambling problem must address what two factors?

Public resistance to tax increases, the political power of gambling interests, and the growing pursuit of easy money have led to the legalization of some form of gambling in the District of Columbia and every state except Utah and Hawaii. An enormous increase in the amount of money Americans are betting has accompanied the wildfire growth of gambling in America. In 1982, Americans bet $125.7 billion on all forms of legal gambling in the U.S. and lost $10.4 billion. In 1998, the amount Americans bet rose to $677.4 billion and the amount they lost exceeded $54.3 billion. It is time to take a closer look at this issue and to develop a response. . . .

While the advocates of legalized gambling promote it as an economic development tool and as a supposedly painless source of tax revenue, there are numerous biblical, ethical, and social reasons why gambling is not an acceptable activity. Below are some of the most obvious reasons.

Gambling Violates Biblical Principles

While the Bible contains no "thou shalt not" in regard to gambling, it does contain many insights and principles which indicate that gambling is wrong. For example, the Bible emphasizes the sovereignty of God over human events (Matt. 10:29–30); whereas gambling looks to chance and luck. The Bible indicates that man is to work creatively and use his possessions for the good of others (Eph. 4:28); gambling fosters a something-for-nothing attitude. The Bible calls for careful stewardship; gambling calls for reckless abandon. The Bible condemns covetousness and materialism (Matt. 6:24–34); gambling has both at its heart. The moral thrust of the Bible is love for God and neighbor (Matt. 22:37–40); gambling seeks personal gain and pleasure at another person's loss and pain.

Gambling Contributes to Crime and Corruption

The growth of crime in those states and cities that legalize gambling is easily demonstrated. [A study in 1999 concluded] that after three or four years, counties with casino gambling experience increases in rape, robbery, aggravated assault, burglary, larceny, and auto theft compared to counties without casinos. Because of their contribution to gambling addiction, lotteries cause increases in crime as well.

Many careful studies on gambling point out frequent incidents of corruption related to gambling. Police are the most immediate targets for corrupting influences. Since police operate at the entry point of the criminal justice system, they are both more available and more desirable as targets of gamblers seeking to make payoffs and bribes. But gambling corruption is by no means limited to the police. Elected officials as well as individuals in the gambling business are also subject to the corrupting influence of gambling.

Organized crime benefits from the expansion of gambling as well. William Webster, a former FBI director, said, "I really don't see how one can expect to run legalized gambling anywhere without serious problems. . . . Anytime organized crime sees an opportunity to put a fix on something, to get an edge on something, it'll be there. And gambling is still the largest source of revenue for organized crime."

Gambling Disrupts the Economy and Destroys Lives

Until recently, business and labor leaders have led many of the successful efforts to prevent gambling from entering states and communities because they realized that gambling is bad for the economy and especially bad for relatively low-income la-

SNAPSHOTS

The only machine in Vegas that pays out.

borers. Unfortunately, many current business and labor leaders have become either neutral or supportive of gambling because of its alleged economic benefits. However, increased gambling always results in increases in unpaid bills, embezzlement, bankruptcy, and absenteeism from jobs. In addition, gambling does not help a state's economy in any appreciable way. A lottery returns to the state an average of only about 32 cents of every dollar taken in. The remainder goes to prizes and administration. In only three or four states does the revenue from lotteries, casinos, pari-mutuel betting, and any other existing forms of gambling contribute more than 3 percent to a state's total budget. The minimal contribution that gambling makes to a state's economy is more than offset by the social and personal problems it creates.

Gambling corrupts and hurts people in many ways. The something-for-nothing craving which gambling stimulates undermines character. The hope of winning a fortune causes some to embezzle and steal for a gambling stake. Gambling appeals to the weakness of a person's character and develops recklessness, callousness, and covetousness. Some gamblers become psychologically addicted to gambling so that they cannot stop gambling and find themselves in a headlong plunge into personal catastrophe.

Gambling harms not only those directly involved in gambling but innocent people as well. Especially vulnerable are members of the gambler's family. Gambling creates financial problems and special tensions in the home. It is difficult to determine whether the gambler or his or her spouse is more physically, mentally, and emotionally damaged by the ravages of a gambling binge. The children of gamblers suffer when a gambling parent loses the money for such necessities as food, rent, clothing, and medicine. They suffer when a gambling parent abandons them in cars, with neighbors, or in gambling daycare centers while they satisfy their gambling addiction. Communities are hurt by the presence of gambling as increasing numbers of people become addicted to gambling and prey on their communities to support their gambling addictions.

Gambling Defies Justification

Among the arguments advanced to justify gambling is the one which says that all of life is a gamble or a risk. But risk-taking in gambling is different from the risks involved in the normal routine of life. The risks in gambling are artificially created. In other ventures, the risk is part of the creative process. For example, the contractor risks labor and capital to build a house and make a profit. Unlike the gambler, he assumes a risk that is necessary to society's economic life, and he relies on more than chance in seeking to make a profit.

It is also argued that some people like to spend their recreation money betting on horses or playing slot machines, just as others prefer to spend theirs for a round of golf or a movie. Gambling obviously provides a kind of recreational excitement for some, but the cost to individuals, families, the economy, and society is too high to justify it.

Resisting Gambling

Seen in this light, gambling is personally selfish, morally irresponsible, and socially destructive. Therefore, gambling must be vigorously resisted. Such resistance requires an understanding of the problem, a workable plan of attack, and a personal commitment to work against gambling.

The gambling problem results from two interrelated factors: (1) Many people have a desire, often a compulsion, to gamble. (2) Most of these people have access to gambling opportunities. The ultimate goal of a plan of action is to control the desire to gamble and eliminate the access to gambling opportunities.

When the desire to get something for nothing and the opportunity to gamble go hand in hand, resistance to one requires resistance to the other. To attempt to eliminate the desire without abolishing the opportunity is to invite failure. It is a matter of record that as gambling becomes more accessible, more people gamble. Thus, legalization is not the answer to the gambling problem. Instead, it is one primary cause of the gambling problem.

Any adequate plan to deal with gambling must be both extensive and comprehensive. It must be extensive enough to include the spiritual, educational, and legal approaches. It must be comprehensive enough to incorporate the family, the world of work, community clubs and organizations, the church, and government.

Evangelization

A vibrant, growing relationship with Jesus Christ is the only adequate basis for a stable personal life and a sound society. Members of Gamblers Anonymous acknowledge that in order to prevent relapse it is necessary to experience certain personality changes within themselves, and that this involves response to spiritual principles in order to make the changes permanent.

Moral arguments, economic self-interest, guilt, shame, and other lesser motivations will not prevail against the gambling urge or solve society's gambling problem.

Education and Rehabilitation

Families, churches, schools, labor unions, businesses, and community organizations can all contribute to an educational program in opposition to gambling. Such education should be specifically designed to result in action. The dangers of gambling should be exposed in such a dramatic way that people will cast it out of their lives and communities. People can be led to understand that it is in their best personal interest to refrain from gambling and that it is in society's best interest publicly to oppose gambling.

For those addicted to gambling, education alone will prove powerless to deal with their problems. They need psychological help. People gamble for many reasons, and no simple and easy solution covers all cases. Pastoral counseling, psychological care, or participation in a group like Gamblers Anonymous can prove helpful. The community and the church can sometimes work together in providing programs to seek out and help the compulsive gambler and his or her family.

Legislation

When gambling opportunities are available, both the reformed gambler and the potential gambler are tempted. Since gambling is corruptive and harmful, concerned citizens should work for laws to control and eliminate gambling. Effective legislation both by the states and by the federal government is needed.

Anti-gambling legislation will be effective only to the extent that it is backed up by effective law enforcement. Legislation without enforcement fails to deter gambling and stimulates disrespect for the law. A responsible public will insist on, and be willing to pay the price for, strict and efficient law enforcement. Further, the courts must be encouraged to take seriously gambling cases and levy appropriate sentences. For genuine gambling addicts, rehabilitation treatment can be far more effective than jail sentences.

│ *"[The gambling] industry, like any other*
│ *industry, makes important economic*
│ *and social contributions to its commu-*
│ *nities."*

Legalized Gambling Benefits Communities

Frank J. Fahrenkopf Jr.

Frank J. Fahrenkopf Jr. is the president and chief spokesperson for the American Gaming Association (AGA), an industry advocacy organization. He argues in the following viewpoint that casinos are major contributors to the economic well-being of communities that host them. As Fahrenkopf states, casino gaming creates tax revenue, and casinos themselves provide much-needed jobs and job benefits for tens of thousands of Americans. This successful combination, Fahrenkopf contends, has prompted many civic leaders to praise the benefits that casinos bring to host communities across the country.

As you read, consider the following questions:

1. As Fahrenkopf reports, what percentage of casino employees used their jobs to get off public assistance?

Frank J. Fahrenkopf Jr., "Gaming Today: The Economic and Social Impact," speech to the Congressional Black Caucus's Annual Legislative Conference, September 22, 2005. Reproduced by permission of the author.

2. What does the author cite as a significant finding of a 2003 study of the casino industry conducted by Price-Waterhouse Coopers?

3. What is the benefit of casinos adding entertainment, restaurants, and shopping facilities to their establishments, according to Fahrenkopf?

Because our industry is entirely transparent, the commercial casino industry's contributions to the economy are a matter of public record. The 445 casinos in 11 states generated nearly 29 billion dollars in gross revenues in 2004. Of that amount, nearly 4.7 billion dollars went toward gaming taxes paid to state and local governments. We're also a labor-intensive business, providing more than 350,000 direct jobs paying more than 12 billion dollars in salaries, including benefits.

Racetrack casinos—or racinos—have witnessed explosive growth over the past few years, and they represent the fastest growing sector on the commercial side of the gaming business. With 23 operational facilities located in seven states, racetrack casinos alone generated nearly 2.9 billion dollars in gross gaming revenue in 2004, which was 30 percent higher than the previous year. Racetrack casinos employed more than 14,000 people in 2004, and generated in excess of 1 billion dollars for state and local governments.

Benefitting Employees and Communities

Rather than just provide jobs, research shows that employment in the commercial casino industry helps improve lives. According to a study of industry employees conducted in the late 1990s, more than 8.5 percent of commercial casino employees across the country reported they had left welfare as a result of their employment, and 16 percent said they had used their casino industry job to get off public assistance. And 63 percent of casino employees said they had better access to healthcare benefits as a result of their employment.

The commercial casino industry also has long been dedicated to diversity in its hiring practices. According to a 2003 study conducted by PriceWaterhouse Coopers, the U.S. commercial casino industry employs more Black executives, more females and more minorities overall than the general U.S. workforce.

Beyond direct employment and revenues, there have been supplemental benefits from the industry as well. Back in 1996, a federal commission mandated by Congress conducted a two-year study of the impact of gambling. According to commission research released in 1999, communities closest to casinos experienced a drop in welfare payments, unemployment rates and unemployment insurance.

The research also refuted many claims previously made against the industry, finding that spending on social services was no different in places closest to casinos than in places farther from casinos. The research also found no link between gambling and bankruptcy or gambling and crime. The U.S. Treasury Department investigated a possible connection between gambling and bankruptcy around the same time and reached a similar conclusion.

When the commission looked at the magnitude of disordered gambling, they found it was not even close to what had been alleged and continues to be alleged today by many gambling opponents. Approximately 1 percent of American adults can be classified as "pathological gamblers," according to the National Research Council of the National Academy of Sciences (NRC) and Harvard Medical School's Division on Addictions.

Contributing to Local Economies

As an economic impact report funded by the federal commission found, "a new casino of even limited attractiveness, placed

Gaming Revenues for 2005	
Industry	**2005 Gross Revenues**
Card Rooms	$1.12 billion
Commercial Casinos	$31.85 billion[1]
Charitable Games and Bingo	$2.33 billion
Indian Casinos	$22.62 billion[2]
Legal Bookmaking	$130.5 million
Lotteries	$22.89 billion
Pari-mutuel Wagering	$3.68 billion
Total	**$84.65 billion**

[1]Amount includes deepwater cruise ships, cruises-to-nowhere and noncasino devices
[2]Amount includes Class II (offering bingo and some card games) and Class III casinos (offering all casino games)

TAKEN FROM: Christiansen Capital Advisors LLC (as reported on American Gaming Association web site).

in a market that is not already saturated, will yield positive economic benefits on net to its host economy." The commission also concluded that, especially in economically depressed communities, casino gambling has demonstrated the ability to generate economic development through the creation of quality jobs.

When you examine the research and look at real examples instead of the theory and economic models concocted by gambling opponents, you will see that this industry, like any other industry, makes important economic and social contributions to its communities.

But don't take my word for it. The true testimony of casino gaming's impact is best evidenced by the opinions of the civic and community leaders who live and work in gaming communities. [In 2005], the AGA commissioned national pollster Peter Hart to conduct a survey of opinion leaders in communities with commercial and racetrack casinos. He interviewed 201 top local decision makers across the country, including mayors, city and county council members, state leg-

islators, police and fire chiefs, school superintendents, economic development officials and other community leaders.
Most of these leaders lived and worked in these areas before
the introduction of casinos, giving them a first-hand and well-
informed view of the effects of casino businesses on their
communities.

The results of this survey underscore what the commission
research and other studies have shown: Elected officials and
civic leaders are strikingly positive about the impact casinos
have had on their communities. They welcome the additional
tax revenue, jobs, secondary economic development, and the
contributions casino gaming makes to the community and
charitable organizations. Fully 58 percent of those surveyed
say that they had a positive initial reaction when casinos were
first proposed in the community. After the casinos opened,
more than 90 percent of those leaders believe the casinos have
either met or exceeded their expectations.

Local opinion leaders highly value the additional tax revenue that casinos have generated for their communities. Fully
73 percent of community leaders say that tax revenue and local development agreements with casinos have allowed their
communities to undertake projects that otherwise would not
have been possible.

Officials who have watched the development of casinos in
their communities have little question that casinos have been
a positive force for other area companies, despite opponents'
claims otherwise. By a margin of more than three to one,
community leaders are more likely to say that casinos have
done more to help rather than hurt other businesses in the
community.

Civic Approval

When asked to evaluate casinos' corporate citizenship in general, more than 8 out of 10 report that casinos are good corporate citizens. But possibly the most telling result of this sur-

vey is that if given the chance to vote again, a full three-quarters of civic leaders and elected officials would vote again to bring casino gaming to their communities.

In terms of acceptability of casino gaming, the general public overwhelmingly concurs with these opinion leaders. Year after year, an average of 8 out of 10 U.S. adults surveyed indicate that casino gaming is an acceptable form of entertainment for themselves or others, according to the AGA's annual State of the States survey.

These attitudes of the public and local community leaders are a clear testament that casino gaming has evolved into a vital part of the mainstream entertainment culture of our country. Gone are the days when people visited casinos only for the gambling. Today, gaming operators are broadening their offerings for customers, providing a complete entertainment experience, with most resorts' attractions actually found off the casino gaming floor—from spas and restaurants to theatrical performances and sporting events. Not surprisingly, more than 50 percent of the revenues made by casino businesses in Las Vegas now come from non-gaming sources. More attractions mean more customers, which translates into more jobs and more economic growth.

And this phenomenon of non-gaming amenities is not unique to Las Vegas. Operators in communities across the country recognize the importance of offering a wide range of entertainment options at their casinos. By a more than two to one margin, U.S. adults say that attractions like shows, restaurants and shopping are more fun for them than the gambling when they visit casinos.

So as you can see, the benefits of casino gaming are well documented through independent research and supported by the attitudes of community opinion leaders and the public. Through employment, economic stimulation and tax contributions as well as through its new focus on providing a total entertainment package for customers, our casino businesses continue to strive to make a positive difference in the communities where we operate.

> *"The introduction of a casino [to a community] appears to produce a few modestly positive effects, a few modestly negative impacts, and, in several areas, no statistically significant effects at all."*

Legalized Gambling Has a Negligible Effect on Communities

Phineas Baxandall and Bruce Sacerdote

In the following viewpoint, Phineas Baxandall and Bruce Sacerdote examine the economic and social impact of casino gambling on U.S. communities in order to offer advice to Massachusetts policy makers who are contemplating the legalization of casinos within the state. According to the authors, casinos have had little positive or negative effect on local economies, showing minor rises in employment opportunities, local revenues, and property values, while revealing equally tepid increases in crime and bankruptcies. Baxandall is the assistant director of the Rappaport Institute for Greater Boston, which provides scholarly research to policy makers and civic leaders. Sacerdote is a professor of economics at Dartmouth College in New Hampshire.

Phineas Baxandall and Bruce Sacerdote, "Betting on the Future: The Economic Impact of Legalized Gambling," Rappaport Institute for Greater Boston Policy Brief, January 13, 2005. www.ksg.harvard.edu/rappaport. Reproduced by permission.

As you read, consider the following questions:

1. According to Baxandall and Sacerdote, what is the average population of a county with a "large" casino?

2. In the authors' findings, what was the average difference in housing prices between counties that hosted casinos and those that did not?

3. What factors do Baxandall and Sacerdote suggest the Massachusetts policy makers should examine when making their decision about whether to allow casino gambling in the state?

For over a decade, advocates and opponents of casinos in the Commonwealth [of Massachusetts] have argued about whether legalized gambling would produce prosperity or ruin. Our analysis—which compares the experience of counties in the United States that house casinos with those that do not—suggests that both sides are wrong.

Instead, the introduction of a casino appears to produce a few modestly positive effects, a few modestly negative impacts, and, in several areas, no statistically significant effects at all. . . .

Methodology

[Our] study focuses [on] the county-level impacts of an Indian-owned casino. [The study examined the impact of 365 Indian casinos located in 156 counties in 26 states.] We analyze the effects of casinos at the county level rather than the state level because entire states are simply too large to discern a casino's influences on outcomes such as employment or crime. Indian casinos are analyzed because of the availability of comprehensive data and because approval of any casino-style gambling facility may enable recognized tribes to open their own casinos in the state.

Standard statistical techniques are used to compare changes in outcomes such as house prices, crime, and local services, in counties that host a casino with counties that do not. The specific techniques are designed to separate the impacts of the casinos on surrounding areas from the impacts of larger trends occurring at the same time. . . .

Population Changes

Casino advocates often argue that by providing economic opportunities, a casino will stem and perhaps reverse population and employment declines in distressed areas. Casino critics, on the other hand, sometimes argue that problems associated with casinos may hasten the exodus from troubled areas.

On average, counties with casinos were home to about 155,000 people, almost two times more than the average U.S. county, which contained approximately 85,000 people. Counties with "large" casinos (more than 1,760 slot machines) were home to 479,000 people, more than five times the population of the average counties.

Casinos also seem to attract new residents. Between 1990 and 2000 the population of counties with casinos grew about 5 percent faster relative to similar counties that did not have a casino. "High-population" casino counties grew about 8 percent faster relative to similar counties without a casino. Population growth in "big-slot" counties, however, was not statistically different than growth in similar counties without casinos. However, although the population of Connecticut's New London County, which has more slot machines than any other county in the country, grew by 1.5 percent in the 1990s, that growth was 3 percent slower than the state average.

Employment Opportunities

Casinos can create jobs by directly employing people to deal cards, serve drinks, maintain order, clean bathrooms, and perform other casino-related tasks. Casinos also can create jobs when they attract patrons from outside the county who spend money at local hotels, gift shops, or other attractions. Employees at local casinos and casino-related businesses may also generate additional jobs if their incomes rise and they spend more at local businesses. On the other hand, if local residents lose money gambling, they may also spend less money at local businesses, reducing employment. Casinos could also reduce local employment (or at least redistribute jobs away from local businesses) if people come to a casino instead of patronizing local businesses.

We found mixed results. Compared to similar counties, the introduction of a casino corresponds to a 6.7 percent increase in the number of people reporting full or part-time employment. Due to population growth, however, the employment rate—the portion of the population with jobs—increased only 1.1 percent.

In more populous casino counties, such as those typically found in Massachusetts, the number of jobs increased 5.7 percent over the decade. Due to population increases, however, the employment rate actually decreased by 1.7 percent. This effect showed by far the strongest level of statistical significance among all the employment findings.

In counties with larger-capacity casinos, total employment increased almost 15 percent faster than similar counties without casinos. While the employment-to-population rate in these counties showed a 2.8 percent increase, this relationship was barely statistically significant and it vanished among the nine large-slot counties that are also large-population counties. In other words, large counties with large casinos showed no change in their employment rate.

Casinos also appear to have a strong—but uneven—impact on employment in our before-and-after comparison of the 16 largest and most urban casino counties. Before these casinos opened, the average employment rate in those counties stood three-quarters of a percentage point lower than the average in their respective states. In the years after at least one casino opened in those counties, the average employment exceeded their respective state averages by about 1 percent. The data is not conclusive, however, as shown by the fact that employment rates in five of these 16 counties did not exceed state averages after those casinos opened.

Unemployment Problems

Casinos seem to produce small and mixed effects on unemployment rates. For all counties, the introduction of a casino did not cause statistically significant differences in unemployment compared to counties without casinos. Among populous counties, those that introduced a casino saw a 0.5 percent higher unemployment rate than those without a casino. However, the unemployment rate in the large-capacity casino counties dropped by 0.6 percent compared to similar counties. And the unemployment rate dropped by 1.2 percent in the nine counties with large populations and large casinos.

In our separate snapshot of the nation's 16 largest-capacity casino counties, we generally found a small reduction in unemployment compared to statewide averages. In 1990, before the introduction of casino gambling, the unemployment rate in these 16 counties was on average 0.1 percent higher than their respective state rates. But in 2001, after casinos had opened, the counties had average unemployment rates that were 0.7 percent lower than their respective state rates. The pattern was not uniform, however, as illustrated by the fact that the unemployment rate in Connecticut's New London County rose 0.1 percent compared to the statewide average after the introduction of casinos.

Home Values

Because population increases in casino counties, it seems likely that house prices in these counties would rise as well. Even if population did not increase, moreover, casinos might make communities more attractive by producing revenues that their host communities could use to improve public services and/or lower residential tax bills. On the other hand, if

Casinos' Impact on Social Aspects and Quality of Life		
Largest U.S. Counties with Tribal Casino	Change in Relative Unemployment (before minus after)	Change in Relative Crime (after minus before)
Aitkin, MN	−0.40%	−10
Allen Parish, LA	−3.20%	3
Attala, MS	−0.90%	−20
Avoyelles Parish, LA	−3.00%	19
Bernalillo, NM	0.00%	−3
Broward, FL	0.70%	−7
Brown, WI	−0.20%	−4
Carlton, MN	0.00%	−5
Cherokee, NC	−1.00%	0
Forest, WI	−0.50%	9
Maricopa, AZ	−1.40%	−4
New London, CT	0.10%	−1
Riverside, CA	−1.40%	−16
San Bernadino, CA	−0.50%	−10
San Diego, CA	−0.40%	−9
Scott, MN	−0.50%	−6

TAKEN FROM: Phineas Baxandall and Bruce Sacerdote, "The Casino Gamble in Massachusetts," Rappaport Institute for Greater Boston working paper, January 13, 2005. www.ksg.harvard.edu/rappaport.

casinos were associated with problems such as crime, traffic congestion, and unmet needs for greater public services, then existing residents might be eager to sell their homes at lower prices.

To sort out temporary and place-specific real-estate trends from the larger effect of casinos on how much people value living in a community, we look at home prices over an extended period and across numerous cases. We use U.S. Census data to compare countywide self-reported median home values from the 1990 Census with median values from the 2000 Census.

This analysis produces mixed results. Within the broadest sample, houses in counties where a casino opened in the 1990s were about 2 percent more expensive than houses in similar non-casino counties, a difference of about $6,000. Casinos in high-population counties, however, had no statistically significant effects on house prices. Similarly, house prices in counties that housed the largest casinos did not grow any faster than house prices in counties without large casinos. And house prices in our snapshot of the 16 largest and most urban casino counties increased at a rate that was 2 percent slower than the average statewide increase in the states where those counties are located.

Crime and Bankruptcy

Communities that consider introducing a casino worry about social problems such as crime and bankruptcy. If casinos substantially increase local incomes and employment, individuals may be less likely to commit crimes or file for bankruptcy. On the other hand, problem gamblers are more likely to have financial problems that lead to bankruptcy and may be more likely to turn to illegal activities as a way to pay debts and support their habit.

Turning first to crime, previous large-scale studies suggest that casinos increase certain kinds of crimes. [William N.] Evans and [Julie H.] Topoleski [economists at the University of Maryland], for example, found that after four years of opening a casino, the total amount of violent crime rate reported in a county increased by 9 percent and property crimes—primarily auto thefts and larcenies—increased by 4.4 percent.

Our analysis shows that while total crime can be expected to increase when casinos open, the increase is due to increased population, not to a casino-created crime wave. Looking at FBI-indexed crimes per resident in all counties, we find that introducing a casino is associated with a decrease of 3 reported crimes per 1,000 people. The introduction of a casino, however, had no statistically significant effect on per-capita crime rates in either large-population casino counties or in large-casino counties. The per-capita crime rate in the 9 large-population counties that also hosted large-capacity casinos dropped 9 crimes per 1,000 residents, however.

Turning to [the issue of] bankruptcy, previous research indicates that proximity to casinos leads to increases in both overall gambling and the incidence of problem gambling. . . .

We also find that proximity to casinos tends to increase personal bankruptcies. Our analysis measures the rate of personal bankruptcies per 1,000 people before and after introducing a casino. The mean in the United States during this period is 2.98 personal bankruptcies per 1,000 people. Looking at all counties that introduced casinos, the effect appears to increase the bankruptcy rate by about 10 percent from 2.98 to 3.27 personal bankruptcies per 1,000 people. In more populous counties the bankruptcy rate rose to 3.44 bankruptcies per 1,000 people. We found no additional statistically significant effects when we looked only at larger casinos. Whether or not these increases are alarming is a matter of judgment. The evidence suggests, for instance, that a casino in southeastern Massachusetts' Bristol County, which had 534,678 residents in 2000, would lead to 246 additional bankruptcies per year.

Revenue and Spending Increases

For many state and local officials, casinos are attractive because they promise to provide significant new revenues at a time when all levels of government face serious fiscal problems. It is difficult, however, to predict the overall fiscal impacts of prospective casinos. The changing legal and political terrain surrounding Indian casinos shifts the bargaining leverage and thus the likely terms of revenue-sharing compacts between states and tribes and any ancillary agreements between tribes and localities. It is also unclear to what extent new casinos in Massachusetts would lead to more gambling or merely redistribute existing patrons—and the revenues they generate for states and localities—among a larger number of facilities.

If casinos spur economic development around gambling facilities, localities near casinos should see rising revenues from increased property-tax revenues, sales taxes, and revenue-sharing agreements from casinos owned by Indian tribes that are exempt from local taxes. On the other hand, casinos and casino-related growth could increase the demand for government services such as policing, roads, and schools.

In fact, casinos had surprisingly little impact on local revenues and expenditures. Specifically, combined total revenues and spending for county and municipal governments in areas that introduced casinos did not increase (or decrease) at rates that were significantly different than areas without casinos. This is true for high-population counties and those with large-capacity casinos as well. . . .

Neither Prosperity nor Ruin

For over a decade, advocates and opponents of casinos in the Commonwealth have argued about whether legalized gambling would produce prosperity or ruin. Our analysis indicates that at the county level—where any positive or negative effects are likely to be concentrated—casinos would have only relatively minor effects. . . .

These findings do not mean that casino gambling is a trivial issue—only that employment, finances, and crime are insufficient rationales for deciding whether to deny or allow casinos in Massachusetts. Policymakers, therefore, must consider other issues when deciding whether to allow casino gambling in the state. These might include questions such as whether (and how) casinos would alter the Commonwealth's character, whether it is problematic to rely on gaming revenues to fund public services; and whether allowing limited casino gambling will compromise the state's ability to control gambling in the future.

> *"Gambling revenue is being used to fund health care, education, law enforcement and other services for Indian people."*

Indian Gaming Benefits Tribes

Dave Palermo

With the passage of the 1988 Indian Gaming Regulatory Act, the U.S. government recognized the right of Indian tribes to operate gaming facilities. Since that time, many tribes have secured "compacts"—legal agreements between state governments and the tribes—that define the types of gambling services offered on reservation land and any fees the tribes will pay to their host states. In the following viewpoint, Dave Palermo describes how Native American tribes in Washington State have benefited from gambling revenues generated through these "compacted" enterprises. Palermo contends that the considerable income from gaming has helped the traditionally impoverished reservations fund education, strengthen local economies, and provide health care and other services for Native Americans. Dave Palermo is a freelance writer and president of Native First Communications, a gaming media consulting firm.

As you read, consider the following questions:

1. According to the National Indian Gaming Association, as cited by Palermo, how many jobs did tribal gaming create in 2005?
2. How has Indian gaming been beneficial to non-Indian communities, according to statistics presented by the Taylor Policy Group, cited by the author?
3. In Palermo's view, why has it been difficult for some tribes to launch successful gaming enterprises?

Growing up on the Quinault Indian Nation in Washington state, Randy Scott recalls the 1960s, when jobs were scarce and poverty weighed heavily on the reservation community of Taholah.

A proud people with a rich culture, the Quinault and other Pacific Northwest Indian tribes were struggling to get federal courts to uphold U.S. fishing treaty rights. Fishing on Quinault is a spiritual practice. Elders voiced concern over vanishing salmon. The old ways, they said, were becoming ways of the past.

"There was little hope," said Scott, director of tribal operations. "There were no jobs. People walked with their heads down. They would not look up."

The situation on Quinault was endemic to most all Indian Country, where federal policies of tribal termination and allotment of Indian land had fostered poverty, stripped Indians of their ancestral territory and crippled tribal governments.

The late Joe DelaCruz, Pearl Capoeman-Baller and other Quinault leaders joined neighboring tribes in a war to protect Indian sovereignty, battles waged on Capitol Hill and in the federal courts. President Richard Nixon in 1970 called for a new federal policy of tribal self-determination. And a landmark U.S. District Court ruling in 1974 eventually upheld 120-year-old treaties granting fishing rights to the Quinault and other coastal tribes.

Meanwhile, Washington native nations became pioneers in tribal self-determination and many were early enrollees in the Self-Governance Demonstration Project of 1988, legislation that enabled tribes to assume control over programs and services previously managed by the Bureau of Indian Affairs. Washington tribes began strengthening their governments and managing fishing, timber and other resources. But without sufficient revenue to provide services to tribal members, economic and social progress was painfully slow.

Improving Tribal Fortunes

Tribal fortunes improved dramatically in 1988 with passage of the Indian Gaming Regulatory Act, legislation that recognized the inherent and legal right of American Indians to engage in gaming on tribal lands.

There are few regions of the country where the impact of Indian gaming has been greater than in Washington state. Quinault Beach Resort and Casino, opened in 2000, has created economic growth, jobs and, most importantly, hope for the native people of Taholah. Half of the 640 resort jobs and most management positions are held by Quinault tribal members. Casino revenue provides health care and other services to the tribe. And resort profits are helping Quinault buy back ancestral lands lost generations ago.

"Since self-governance and the resort, people who would walk staring at the ground now walk with their heads up, and they have smiles on their faces," Scott said. "They're paying for a new car. They've got clothes for the kids, food on the table. I see a pride in the community we didn't have before."

Indian gaming [in 2005] generated $22.6 billion in tribal revenue nationwide while creating 600,000 jobs, according to the National Indian Gaming Association. Gambling revenue is being used to fund health care, education, law enforcement and other services for Indian people.

Keeping Reservation Communities Intact

Since 1950, North Dakotans from rural areas have been moving into towns and cities or leaving the state altogether. . . .

Indian nations are the exception to North Dakota's rural population shift, largely because of the positive impacts of Indian gaming. Tribal and reservation populations are growing and the growth in population is the youngest in all of North Dakota. Indian gaming is providing the employment opportunities to keep young people at home and Indian gaming revenues are financing the basic infrastructure necessary to re-build and sustain rural reservation communities. Carl Walking Eagle, Vice Chairman and Gaming Commission[er] at Spirit Lake [Nation], says that gaming not only allows people to live at home, but to thrive there. He observes that tribal members "have a new sense of pride, renewed energies and hope that extends a sense of satisfaction to our elders, and instills purpose and dedication in our young people."

Kate Spilde, "Indian Gaming in North Dakota: Resisting the Exodus,"
November 2000.

In Washington state [in 2005], 27 tribes operating casinos or leasing slot machines generated $1.3 billion, according to Analysis Group Inc. Revenue not going to governmental services is being reinvested in upscale resort hotels, shopping malls, construction businesses and other enterprises intended to diversify tribal portfolios. The Quinault facility is one of nearly a dozen tribal resorts now operating or in the planning stages.

Washington tribal governments, their casinos and other business enterprises in 2004 generated $2.2 billion and employed 17,500 people, according to a survey by Taylor Policy

Group of Cambridge, Mass. Group President Jonathan Taylor said individual Indians in the state in 2004 owned 5,731 companies that generated an additional $1 billion in revenue and employed 11,500 people.

Economic growth on Indian reservations is also having a major impact on surrounding non-Indian communities. About 75 percent of tribal jobs arc held by non-Indians, Taylor said. And the overall tribal economy in 2004 generated $141 million in local and state taxes.

Tribal gambling in Washington state ranks sixth nationwide in terms of gross revenues and its impact on the state economy is, indeed, significant. But the role of gambling in strengthening the governmental, social and cultural development of Washington tribes is even more impressive.

Money to Fund Civic Growth

"Steady growth in Indian gaming . . . has allowed tribes to invest in socioeconomic recovery at levels never before possible," Taylor said. "In Washington, as elsewhere, tribal spending has spanned a range of government functions including healthcare, education and childcare, natural resource management, housing, public works and administration, social services and more.

"As casino revenues have placed new resources at their disposal, tribes have seized opportunities for extending and enhancing self-government. Legally speaking, many of these opportunities have been available since as early as the mid-1970s. Practically, however, such opportunities were impossible to seize until adequate tribal government income became available."

Launching gaming enterprises has proven difficult in many states where tribes lacked sufficient governmental structures. Some tribes negotiating federally mandated gaming agreements, or compacts, with state officials entered into onerous revenue-sharing commitments or ceded jurisdiction over tribal lands to local and state agencies, decisions that eroded tribal sovereignty. Others found it difficult to create casino regulatory agencies. Controversies grew over tribal enrollment and per capita payment of casino profits to tribal members.

But decades devoted to building their governments left Washington tribes well-equipped to integrate casino gambling into an overall strategy for economic development and political, social and cultural preservation.

The Puyallup Tribe near Tacoma was recently cited by the National Indian Gaming Commission for excessive per capita payments to tribal members, a claim tribal leaders vigorously deny. But otherwise there has been little controversy over Indian gaming in Washington, and most tribes are using gaming revenues to provide government services and build tribal business enterprises. . . .

Planning to Increase Services on the Reservation

Attorney Fawn Sharp, serving her first term as president of the Quinault Tribal Council, hopes to create a comprehensive program to combat methamphetamine abuse on the reservation, one which will require pooling the resources of health clinicians, law enforcement, family service counselors, state agencies and others.

She also wants to accelerate efforts to reacquire ancestral lands. Only about 32 percent of Quinault's 220,000-acre reservation is under tribal government ownership, much of it having been lost as a result of federal allotment of tribal lands. "I want to see that reach 51 percent in my lifetime," she said, a goal that will enable the tribe to increase its timber industry.

Finally, Sharp hopes to develop a plan for tribal revenue generation that includes a comprehensive system of taxation and policies to attract business and industry to the reservation.

"Tribes today are being placed in a position of trying to generate revenue from commercial ventures," Sharp said. "But we are nations, first and foremost. We need to preserve and protect our ability to generate sustainable revenue for the future to provide important governmental services to our people."

Those goals are more attainable with revenue from gaming.

"With tribal government dollars you have the ability to fund priorities, to develop concentrated efforts to meet the needs of our communities and our nation," Sharp said. "That's the attractive thing about generating profits from gaming. Its one area where tribes can use tribally generated resources to, for instance, match categorical funding—grant funding—to create more opportunity for the nation. . . .

"We are an entire generation removed from the fishing rights controversy and the Boldt decision," Sharp said of the 1974 ruling by U.S. District Judge George Boldt affirming tribal treaty rights to 50 percent of the salmon harvest in Washington state. The ruling was later upheld by the U.S. Supreme Court.

"Those victories and court decisions reaffirming our right to regulate our lands laid the foundation for a positive view toward our future," Sharp said. "I think there is more optimism within the tribal community. I hope it continues."

> "What American people don't understand . . . is the devastation wrought by introducing gambling into a society already crippled by alcoholism and poverty."

Indian Gaming Hurts Tribes

Candi Cushman

Candi Cushman is an associate editor of Citizen *magazine, a publication of the Christian organization Focus on the Family. In the following viewpoint, Cushman describes the resistance to Indian gaming among some of the Navajo people of the American Southwest. Through interviews with prominent leaders and local residents of the Navajo Nation—which had at that time not adopted gaming on reservation land—Cushman reveals that many Navajo were concerned about the negative consequences gambling might bring. According to these spokespeople, gambling addiction might cripple a nation already living with poverty and alcoholism. They also cautioned that the supposed economic benefits have not appeared for other gaming tribes in the region and therefore would likely not materialize for the Navajo should the tribal nation sanction gaming. In 2004 the Navajo did vote to adopt gambling on the reservation and casinos were expected to be built in 2006.*

As you read, consider the following questions:

1. In Edison Wauneka's view, as cited by Cushman, what kinds of people does he fear will become regular customers of Indian casinos?

2. According to the author, what did the October 2001 gambling ordinance allow individual Navajo tribes to do?

3. To what does Richard Delores attribute the collapse of resistance to gaming among the Laguna tribe in New Mexico, according to Cushman?

Some call it America's Third World, this forgotten land of strange, mythic rock formations that jut dramatically from the ground, where towering red cliffs are interspersed with dilapidated wooden shacks, occasional tepees and lonely trailers. It seems such a strange contrast—this abject poverty in the midst of majestic creation, with its telltale signs of a culture in decline: bright yellow "don't drink, don't drive" signs and tiny white crosses marking drunken-driving accidents dotting the highway every few miles.

Welcome to the Navajo Nation, an enchanting yet tragic land, whose 298,000 tribe members—more than half spread over a 17-million-acre land mass roughly the size of West Virginia—have struggled for centuries to overcome poverty, addiction and fragmented families. But now some people say they have found the Navajos' salvation: casinos.

"More senior citizens get quality health care, more children can afford a college education . . . and every Indian tribe has equal opportunity," promised pro-gambling commercials that accosted Arizona television viewers [in 2002]. Against a backdrop of sunny-faced Native American children, plaintive elderly men and young families, the ad urged voters to support efforts to expand gambling over the next two decades because "our future demands nothing less."

Similar emotional, quick-money pitches intended to guilt-trip communities into approving Indian casinos have successfully spread through Louisiana, California and New York in recent years. But those behind this latest advertising blitz have neglected to mention an important fact: The majority of voters in the Navajo Nation—America's largest Indian tribe, covering New Mexico, Arizona and Utah—oppose gambling. So much so, they voted it down twice.

During a trip across the Southwest, *Citizen* met these voters—an array of Native Americans that includes housewives, tribal leaders and former medicine men—who believe gambling will destroy, not save, their people.

Another Addiction

It's 10 A.M. on Friday, and 88 Navajo Council delegates have assembled at the tribe's Capitol in Window Rock, Ariz.—named for a huge sandstone rock that, like a giant peephole into the sky, is punctured with a perfectly eroded circle. Beside the rock sits the Navajo Council Chamber, a round stone fort.

Inside, Delegate Edison Wauneka, chairman of the Navajo Public Safety Committee, complains that casino ads give Native Americans a one-sided view of gambling: "What we don't get is the other side, the dark side—what's happening to the families, people addicted to it, the children. The government is not making that known to the people; they are trying to cover that up."

While gambling advocates promise new jobs and better health care at the expense of rich white tourists, Wauneka sees a different reality. He sees it in the lines of elderly Navajos with Social Security checks in their pockets and single moms hoping for extra rent money who greet off-reservation casino buses at dawn. He sees it in the faces of Indian children confiscated by social services whose mothers left them to play the slots. And he sees it in the fathers addicted to gambling who have started trickling into the tribe's addiction-recovery offices.

Add to that the scourge of alcoholism—as evidenced by the victims of alcohol-related accidents featured weekly in the *Navajo Times*' obituary section. According to a study released [in] December [2001] by New York's [State] University at Buffalo Research Institute on Addictions, problem drinkers are 23 times more likely to have a gambling problem. The study also found that pathological gambling is "significantly higher among minorities and lower-income individuals," which doesn't bode well for Navajos, since at least 50 percent of them depend on welfare.

What American people don't understand, explains Milton Shirleson—a one-time Navajo medicine man turned Christian pastor—is the devastation wrought by introducing gambling into a society already crippled by alcoholism and poverty. Decades of welfare dependency and addiction have steadily ravaged his people, and now Shirleson fears gambling will strike the final blow.

"A lot of our Navajo people go to the border casinos, and they mix that with alcohol," Shirleson says. "The husband gambles his money away, comes home, the money is tight, there's an argument and the guy goes drinking and domestic violence increases. . . . It's increasing because gambling is so accessible."

Standing beside a wooden church sign depicting an open Bible and the verse "The truth will set you free," Shirleson says he has counseled roughly 150 Indian families hurt by gambling addictions: "The first monster I call alcoholism has swept our people. Now there is a second monster our government is trying to release—gambling." . . .

Bowing to Pressure

[In spring 2002], Arizona Gov. Jane Dee Hull pushed for legislative approval of a compact allowing unprecedented gambling expansion in exchange for more state regulation and an estimated $83 million state share in casino profits—despite a federal judge's ruling that governors don't have the power to bind the state in tribal gambling deals. After their proposal failed, Hull and leaders from 17 tribes joined forces to get the compact on the November [2002] ballot.

Feeling the pressure, Navajo leaders signed an ordinance [in] October [2001] allowing individual tribe chapters (political entities similar to states) to seek exemption from tribal gambling prohibitions—even though thousands of Navajos like Shirleson voted down casinos during reservation-wide referendums in 1994 and 1997. So far, leaders of at least three chapters have requested exemptions, spurring fears that gambling will spread across the reservation.

"It's already been a problem with all the casinos surrounding the area," says 57-year-old Jerry Gohns, a member of To'hajiilee, the first Navajo chapter allowed an exemption. Of the eight employees Gohns oversees as transportation director at the chapter high school, "seven are going [gambling]," he says. "When they get paid, the following week they ask to borrow money—even just three dollars. That's how bad it is."

A few miles away, one of the nation's oldest Indian pueblos, Laguna, offers ominous foreshadowing of where the Navajos could be headed. Like the Navajo Nation, Laguna once forbade gambling and alcohol; but now the pueblo, a rustic collection of adobe homes and ranches near Albuquerque, N.M., has two new casinos and a grocery aisle full of beer and wine.

"We stood against gambling for the longest time," says Richard Delores, a Laguna native whose grandfather was a tribal high priest. "I can remember saying, 'This tribe will never give in to gaming; this tribe will stand.'

"But little by little, some of the old folks died out and some younger ones came into political positions, and the foundation crumbled."

Corruption in Indian Gaming

Thanks to one of the industry's biggest regulatory loopholes, there is no single independent body to audit Indian casino finances. Nor are tribal casinos required to disclose financial information, either to the public or to their members. The watchdog National Indian Gaming Commission (NIGC) is privy to some data but, citing tribal sovereignty protection, won't make it public. Native Americans who try to expose corruption, including many of the Kickapoo, have been threatened with reprisals by tribal leaders. Federal agencies sometimes respond to their complaints; more often, they do nothing. But one thing is consistent: the victims tend to be the poorest of the Indians.

Donald L. Bartlett et al.,
Time, *December 23, 2002.*

Casinos Draw Local Customers

An obnoxious gold-shaped dome that seems an affront to the serene red cliffs behind it, the Laguna-owned Dancing Eagle Casino uses a gleaming white Nissan draped with a "Win Me" banner to attract customers. You can only win the car by betting, Delores says, as he waves to a cousin driving a casino bus and then greets a man gambling inside who works for the tribe's housing department. The man is surrounded by other Native Americans sitting in a dark, smoke-filled room, spellbound by multi-colored slot machines. The only visible Caucasians are two truck drivers and a retired couple.

Just down the road is the pueblo's other casino, The Laguna Travel Center, where fields of red dirt are being cleared for 1,000 slot machines, a golf course and RV parking lots. Despite the construction, a hastily erected box-like structure tempts locals with 95 slot machines. Inside, an elderly Navajo couple with sunken eyes and withered faces confess they come here often because "our nation doesn't allow it."

"We never win," admits the wife, with quiet resignation. But before she can reveal how much they've lost that day, a security guard escorts *Citizen* outside for asking too many questions.

Yet statistics reveal what casinos work so hard to hide. Like the fact that most nonmetropolitan gambling operations draw most of their customers from a 35- to 55-mile radius, according to the U.S. Gambling Study conducted by the University of Massachusetts at Amherst. "When you have that kind of impact, you are not bringing in new dollars. You are drawing out money from local enterprises," says the study's director, Robert Goodman.

And even though casinos lure locals, the profits have yet to translate into big bucks for Laguna tribe members, says Delores, who was offered a job at the casino for $6 an hour—half of what he makes as a pesticide man. Meanwhile, some of the community benefits promised by gambling promoters—like more prison space—have yet to materialize two years into the casino's operation.

Few Employment Opportunities

Delores, who gets inside access to spray both casinos, is also bothered by the fact that he never sees Indian managers. "They said they would train people . . . but when a nontribal person comes in with skills and money, he gets the top position."

His observations are on target: The National Indian Gaming Association told *Citizen* that "of the 300,000 jobs provided by 321 Indian gambling operations nationwide, 75 percent are held by non-Indians. And although Indian gambling has skyrocketed since 1990, the vast majority of American Indians . . . have not realized the early 'high hopes' of the casino boom," according to an Associated Press computer analysis of unemployment, poverty and public-assistance records released in September 2000.

One of the only studies of its kind, the analysis found that unemployment on reservations stayed at about 54 percent between 1991 and 1997 despite the casino boom. "Overall, the new [casino] jobs have not reduced unemployment for Indians," concluded the report, adding that only casinos near major cities have thrived while "most others have little left after paying the bills."

Effect on Families

None of this surprises Delores. "You always heard at village meetings, 'It's good money; look at all the money we are going to be getting from truck drivers and tourists,'" he says. "But in my heart I knew this was poison coming in."

And now he sees that poison in the faces of friends and neighbors—like the Laguna family living in a tiny brick and clay home tucked behind a windswept mesa. The mother, Cindy, stands at the kitchen window, gazing blankly at dust devils swirling outside. A physical therapist who works at the local hospital and supports three teenage daughters, she is obviously an intelligent woman. But Cindy can't figure out how to help her husband overcome his gambling addiction.

"I've tried everything; I've tried taking him to court. . . I've given him so many chances," she says. The final straw came a few nights ago when her husband lost yet another paycheck at the casino. They fought—hard—and Cindy decided to give up.

"I'm filing for divorce this week," she says, pointing out the window toward the Laguna Travel Center. "He just goes right down the road here. What they say is true; gambling breaks up families. He's lost all respect from the kids, and I lost all trust in him."

Outside, her husband, who declines to give his first name, is equally dejected. "I've got a good wife, healthy children, and they don't respect me anymore," he says, staring at the ground. "I can't describe it; it hurts too much."

It all started the night four years ago he won $5,000 at a casino. "It seems like after that I just can't quit. . . . I just blame myself," he says, never looking up as he rakes the yard with angry, jerking motions. "I don't know what's gotten into me. I'm not the same person anymore. The problem is, I know my paycheck's going to be there the next week."

A few feeble-minded addicts like this shouldn't be allowed to spoil gambling benefits for the whole tribe, argue casino backers who justify their profit-from-the-weakest philosophy by promising funding for addiction-recovery programs.

But gambling's social costs far outweigh any economic benefit, according to Navajo financial analyst Richard Kontz. While working for the Navajo Economic Development Division in 1997, he examined proposals for 10 on-site casinos and concluded they were a raw deal.

"They said they would create 3,000 jobs. But when you consider that unemployment is anywhere from 46 to 50 percent, to create 3,000 jobs from gambling would only reduce that rate by 1 percent. And yet think of all the headaches we would bring on—increased alcoholism, increased domestic abuse, increased child neglect. All those increased social problems and the cost of dealing with addicts—it doesn't balance out."

Periodical Bibliography

The following articles have been selected to supplement the diverse views presented in this chapter.

Tresa Baldas	"Is It Gambling If It's Not Real? Attorney Takes on ESPN and Others over Fantasy Sports Leagues," *Recorder*, August 18, 2006.
Greg Beato	"Sin Cities on a Hill: How Legalized Gambling Moved from the Strip to Main Street," *Reason*, May 2006.
Connecticut Law Tribune	"It's Time to Expand Casino Gambling," October 17, 2005.
Jim Doyle	"Backlash on Betting: Californians Have Second Thoughts About Gambling," *San Francisco Chronicle*, October 24, 2004.
Alicia Hansen	"Lotteries Are Another State Tax—but with Better Marketing," *Crain's Chicago Business*, January 3, 2005.
Steve Hirsch	"Casinos Eye Profits Overseas," *Washington Times*, October 13, 2006.
Natalie Hoare	"Building on the Past, Gambling on the Future," *Geographical*, October 2006.
Alexandra Marks	"How Gambling Can Affect Family Finances," *Christian Science Monitor*, April 8, 2005.
Matthew Miller	"Off the Reservation," *Forbes*, June 20, 2005.
Francine Russo	"Ante Up, Ladies: As Poker Mania Grips the Nation, More Women Are Mastering the Game, Applying Their Own Life Lessons to Poker and the Lessons of Poker to Life," *Time*, October 31, 2005.
Peter Scheer	"Indian Burn," *Slate*, November 3, 2003. www.slate.com.

OPPOSING
VIEWPOINTS®
SERIES

CHAPTER 2

How Should the U.S. Government Respond to Internet Gambling?

Chapter Preface

In October 2006 President George W. Bush signed the Safe Port Act into law after it won approval by both the House of Representatives and the Senate. The president outlined the primary aim of the bill, which is the protection of American ports against the threat of terrorist attack. The final section of the bill, a rider titled the Unlawful Internet Gambling Enforcement Act, was not mentioned in the speech. The Unlawful Internet Gambling Enforcement Act, based on the previously unsigned bills of congressmen Bob Goodlatte and Jim Leach, provides legislative grounds that define Internet gambling as illegal and allow for the prosecution of individuals for related crimes within the United States.

Only a month and a few days after the bill was signed into law, twenty-seven individuals were arrested in New York for illegal gaming, becoming the first to face charges following the passage of this bill. Previously the U.S. government had relied solely on the 1961 federal Interstate Wire Act as the basis for prosecuting individuals on Internet gambling charges. Many observers argued, however, that this act was outdated, especially when applied to gambling that occurred on the Internet, a form of communication that did not exist when the original act was written. Other critics believe that the specific intent of the Wire Act was to curb sports betting. The wording of the law, for example, cites the illegality of wire transmissions in relation to gambling on a "sporting event or contest." This phrase has become the subject of debate; although government prosecutors have argued that "sporting" modifies only the term *event*, leaving "contest" to include all other forms of gaming—including Internet wagering. Because of the confusion, however, the government was initially not quick to proceed with indictments under the Wire Act.

The passage of the Unlawful Internet Gambling Enforcement Act has certainly strengthened the government's arsenal against Internet gambling. Yet just before the passage of the bill, federal authorities were showing a greater willingness to make their position clear. In July 2006 David Carruthers, CEO of the Internet gambling Web site BetOnSports.com, was arrested while waiting in Dallas, Texas, for a flight that would take him to the company's headquarters in Costa Rica. Carruthers, a British citizen, was arrested on charges of conspiracy, racketeering, and fraud in relation to the sports betting services of BetOnSports.com. Prior to Carruthers's arrest, many questioned the right of the U.S. government to arrest an individual who is not a citizen of the United States for conducting a business based outside of the United States that operates in accordance with the laws of its homeland. After the indictment of Carruthers and eleven other people with ties to the site—including its founder Gary Stephen Kaplan—it became clear that the U.S. government would exercise its prerogative to arrest and charge those who provided illegal sports betting services to American citizens, even if only on the Internet.

Despite the Carruthers arrest and the signing of the Unlawful Internet Gambling Enforcement Act, debate continues over whether it is the government's role to police Internet gambling. On the one hand, those who favor a ban on Internet gambling argue that negative societal consequences will ensue if the government does not restrict it. Those who oppose such restriction, on the other hand, argue that regulation, not prohibition, of Internet gambling is the proper course the government should pursue. In the following chapter, select authors debate the need for government intervention in this newest arena of gaming in America.

> "Illegal Internet gambling is a plague that threatens every young person in America."

Internet Gambling Should Be Banned to Protect Children

Spencer Bachus

In the following viewpoint, Alabama congressman Spencer Bachus argues that Internet gambling should be eradicated to protect America's youth. He claims that young people have easy access to gambling Web sites and the credit cards needed to wager on these sites. He also warns that young people have extra time on their hands to spend in front of Internet gambling sites, potentially increasing their risk for becoming problem gamblers. The congressman worked with other congressional representatives to introduce H.R. 556, the Unlawful Internet Gambling Funding Prohibition Act, in 2001. This bill was a forerunner to H.R. 4411, the Unlawful Internet Gambling Enforcement Act, which was signed into law by President George W. Bush in 2006.

As you read, consider the following questions:

1. What percentage of eighteen- to twenty-four-year olds use computers for entertainment, according to the report by *American Demographics* cited by the author?

Spencer Bachus, "Don't Bet on It: Internet Gambling a Growing Threat," Representative Press Release, October 15, 2002.

2. How much did each of the two college students cited by Bachus lose by gambling on the Internet?

3. How does the author propose to end Internet gambling?

What would you do if you learned someone was building a casino next door to your house and had invited your children in to gamble?

Well, the news is worse than that. There's a child-accessible casino that's sitting on the computer desk in your den or your child's bedroom. It's not only offering the user an invitation to gamble through games or sports betting, it also spews out pornography and even child pornography.

What may surprise most is that this type of Internet gambling is illegal in the United States. Because of that, virtual casinos are set up by criminals to operate beyond the reach of U.S. law or state laws from so-called offshore or foreign locations.

Illegal Internet gambling is a plague that threatens every young person in America. Don't take my word for it. Dr. Howard Shaffer, director of addiction studies at Harvard University, likens the threat of online gambling to crack cocaine in its potential to destroy young lives.

And far worse, his analysis only calculates the damage from serious gambling addiction. Feed into this analysis that it is not only infecting children and adults alike with a serious gambling addiction, but because these rogue websites routinely offer links to pornography and other morally corrupt sites not appropriate for anyone, and certainly not for our children, the damages are multiplied catastrophically.

Threatens Those Who Use Technology Most

We have all marveled at how adept our children or grandchildren are with computers. [In 2000], the publication *American Demographics* reported that while only one in 10 citizens 65 and older use computers for hobbies and entertainment, seven out of ten 18- to 24-year-olds do so. An estimated 72 percent of 18- to 24-year-olds spend four hours a day on the computer. They can spend hours on the Internet or playing video games, totally losing track of time and those around them.

Now, suppose that instead of playing a harmless game, they were on the computer at one of thousands of Internet gambling sites. Then, imagine that they had your credit card.

In 1995 these unregulated offshore Internet gambling sites were virtually non-existent. Today [in 2002] despite laws in all 50 states prohibiting these activities, $1.6 billion in wagers are placed—that's 1600 million dollars in bets. As gambling on the Internet explodes, children have access to gambling, pornography and who knows what else every day across America. At the click of a mouse, virtual casinos appear on computer screens in dorm rooms and homes. All that's required to play is a credit card number and time. Our young people increasingly have both. Almost 80 percent of college students have credit cards and nearly a third have four or more credit cards. With more than 1,500 gambling sites on the Internet, it's just a matter of time before young people find one.

Ruined Lives

Many already have. A representative of the National Collegiate Athletic Association [NCAA] testified before Congress that Internet gambling is becoming an unmanageable problem on college campuses. Gambling addiction among college students, including athletes, is growing at three times the rate of the adult population. Many students are piling up enormous credit card debts gambling from their dorm room computers. In its testimony, the NCAA played a videotaped account of one student who lost $10,000 gambling over the Internet in three months. In another case, a student lost $5,000 on a single Internet wager on the Super Bowl and was forced to drop out.

Internet Gambling Negatively Affects Sports

Internet gambling has tainted amateur and professional sports. The integrity of the outcome is essential to sporting events and to the credibility of the organizations that sponsor them. Athlete involvement in gambling can compromise that integrity. As [a 2003] *USA Today* article makes clear, there have been several recent examples of amateur and professional athletes heavily involved in sports gambling. Washington Capitals hockey star Jaromir Jagr admitted [in June 2003] to running up a $500,000 debt betting on sports events. In addition, former Florida State quarterback Adrian McPherson pleaded no-contest [in July 2003] to charges of betting on college and professional sports, including his own games. While there is no evidence that either player altered the outcome of a game for gambling purposes, such actions are not uncommon. For instance, a 1998 University of Michigan study found that 35 percent of 758 student-athletes surveyed had gambled on sports and that 5 percent of the males had either provided inside information for gambling purposes, bet on their own sporting events, or accepted money to play poorly. The problem is considered serious enough that major U.S. pro sports leagues and the NCAA [National Collegiate Athletic Association] support legislation blocking payments to online gambling operations.

U.S. Senate Republican Policy Committee, September 3, 2003.

The easy access to illegal Internet casinos is often an irresistible draw—not only to our young people but to Americans of all ages. More than 15 million are addicted to gambling. With Internet gambling on the rise, that number will surely increase. This addiction hurts more than just the gambler. Problem gambling results in broken families, bankruptcy, crime and higher rates of suicide. Unlike "traditional" gambling, Internet gambling comes right into our homes, and thus carries an even greater ability to hurt a wider segment of the population.

As if the negative impact on our children, families and communities wasn't enough, the FBI has testified that unlawful and unsupervised Internet gambling sites serve as a "powerful vehicle" for money laundering activities that can be exploited by terrorists to finance attacks on innocent Americans.

A Bill to Stop Internet Gambling

In response, I have joined others in Congress to introduce legislation to stop illegal Internet gambling. This bill is H.R. 556, the Unlawful Internet Gambling Funding Prohibition Act. It would prohibit the use of any bank instrument—such as a credit card, check or electronic funds transfer—for gambling online. The people who create these sites do it for one reason and one reason only—money. Take the financial incentives away and it stops. For all practical purposes, this bill would put an end to Internet gambling.

As Chairman of the Financial Institutions and Consumer Credit Subcommittee, I have worked to make this bill a priority. . . .

Illegal Internet gambling has reached epidemic proportions. Increasingly, it is putting our youth at greater risk, exacerbating pathological gambling, and opening the door for fraud and money laundering. It is a threat to our nation and must be stopped. . . .

| "If lawmakers do not aggressively com-
bat the growth of Internet gambling,
the effects on our economy will be damaging."

Internet Gambling Should Be Curbed to Protect the Economy

Ryan D. Hammer

In the following viewpoint, Ryan D. Hammer argues for strict control of Internet gambling, which would reduce the potential growth of the industry and in return protect the U.S. economy from many of the negative consequences associated with this growth. After outlining these consequences—including lost tax revenue, consumer credit card problems, and social concerns— Hammer advocates government legislation as a possible solution to the problem. One course of action he suggests would be to limit the use of consumer credit cards in making online gambling wagers. Such legislation was proposed in bill H.R. 4411, which President George W. Bush signed into law in October 2006. Hammer was a graduate student at Indiana University at the time this paper was published.

Ryan D. Hammer, "Does Internet Gambling Strengthen the U.S. Economy? Don't Bet on It," *Federal Communications Law Journal*, vol. 54, October 31, 2001, pp. 117–27. Reproduced by permission.

As you read, consider the following questions:

1. Why is Internet gambling a loss to states, according to Hammer?
2. Who are the biggest losers when credit cards are used for online gambling, in the author's opinion?
3. What percentage of online gamblers does Hammer say make wagers using credit cards?

The recent explosion of Internet gambling poses serious concerns to the U.S. economy. With the U.S. economy slowing significantly after a decade of expansion [in the 1990s] the impact of Internet gambling will be detrimental. One effect will be the reduction in tax revenues collected by state and federal governments from legalized gambling operations. The gambling industry in America represents a significant source of tax revenues to the various jurisdictions in which gambling operates. A second area that will be affected by the Internet gambling phenomenon is the consumer credit card industry. Thirdly, Internet gambling harms families, leads to crime, and increases addiction. Although difficult to quantify, these areas of concern will negatively impair the economy.

Internet Gambling Reduces Tax Revenue

Legal gambling operations in the United States pay millions of dollars in taxes annually to local and federal governments. Without question, these taxes contribute to the overall revenues in the vast majority of states with legalized gambling. [According to journalist Patrick Strawbridge] "State and local governments in Iowa collected more than $197 million in taxes and fees from Iowa casinos and racetracks [in 2000]." The Casino Queen Riverboat in East St. Louis generates between $10 million and $12 million annually in tax revenues for the city. In addition, the riverboat casino created more than 1,200 full-time jobs. "Gaming revenues have enabled the city to make dramatic strides in its quality of life," [states professor Kenneth M. Reardon.] The willingness of states to legalize certain forms of gambling, such as lotteries, often hinges on revenue shortfalls of their treasuries. During the 1980s, sixteen of the twenty-two states with the greatest increase in unemployment created lotteries. It is always easier for politicians to support a lottery or a casino riverboat than to propose a tax increase on their constituents.

When Americans participate in Internet gambling, however, no state budget receives a windfall of revenues. The money gambled by Americans on the Internet is done so with companies that pay no taxes in the United States. With over $2 billion gambled on the Internet in 2000, the amount of tax revenues that the United States loses is staggering. Included in this loss of revenues are secondary items purchased when one attends a gambling facility, such as food, souvenirs, and clothing. . . .

While any gambler desires to win money, the depression of losing can be somewhat alleviated when the money is being reinvested to improve the economy. This is the case when people lose money in regulated gambling environments. For example, when an individual buys a lottery ticket at a convenience store, a portion of the cost of that ticket will be used to improve education or to build better roads. When an individual plays an online lottery, the proceeds are not reinvested to improve any government projects. Legal gambling operations are permitted to function in the United States when they comply with strict regulations such as accounting procedures. No such procedures exist in the world of Internet gambling, which deprives the United States of millions of dollars annually in tax revenues.

Internet Gambling Threatens Credit-Card Industry

Internet gambling places banks and credit card companies in a precarious position. On the one hand, these institutions can profit greatly by offering credit to individuals to gamble on-line. Credit card charges for Internet gambling are often posted as cash advances, which carry higher interest rates than ordinary purchases. The cash advance rate for most credit cards exceeds 20%. The downside to credit card companies stems from the processing of Internet gambling transactions. Numerous lawsuits are filed by individuals who have lost money gambling online and who refuse to pay their gambling debts. These lawsuits could leave banks unable to collect debts from individuals who partake in Internet gambling. . . .

The biggest losers with respect to the use of credit cards in Internet gambling transactions are those who do not gamble online. Regardless of how the litigation evolves in cases of Internet gamblers against credit card companies, the ordinary American loses. If Internet gamblers are successful in having their debts alleviated, non-Internet gamblers will ultimately pay the economic price for their fellow Americans' victory. This price will come in the form of higher fees, charges, and interest rates passed on to all American credit card holders. Because the number of those in the non-Internet gambling community far outweighs the number of those who gamble online, a vast majority of Americans will experience the negative effects of credit card use in Internet gambling transactions.

Even if credit card companies are successful in litigation against Internet gamblers, Americans will still feel negative effects. Victories for credit card companies would provide credibility to the Internet gambling industry and encourage more people to participate. The result of this certification of the Internet gambling industry would cause more and more people to accumulate large Internet gambling debts. When the factor of gambling addiction is added, inevitably many individuals would assume debts unrecoverable to credit card companies. Once again, higher interest rates and fees will be passed on to non-Internet gamblers as a result of the use of credit cards in Internet gambling transactions.

Internet Gambling Is a Problem in the Workplace

Internet gambling at work has become a concern for many employers. A survey conducted [in 2002] by Websense Inc., a San Diego company that supplies Internet-blocking software to businesses, found that 8 percent of employees admitted to finding Internet gambling potentially addictive, and 2 percent admitted to gambling online at the office. These percentages are in line with numerous studies showing that roughly 5 percent of the adult American population has problems with compulsive gambling.

Gregory M. Lamb, Christian Science Monitor, *January 21, 2003.*

Internet Gambling Disrupts Society

The societal concerns that led to the intense regulation of traditional forms of gambling do not disappear when dealing with Internet gambling. As Internet gambling invades American households, society is "left to deal with the crime, bankruptcy, and gambling disorders that may result," [argues Rhodes College professor Michael Nelson]. Among the many problems exacerbated by Internet gambling are gambling addiction and gambling by minors. Pathological gambling negatively affects not only the gambler, but also the gambler's family and friends, and society at large. Societal costs of pathological gambling includes the expenditure of unemployment benefits, physical and mental health problems, theft, embezzlement, bankruptcy, suicide, domestic violence, and child abuse and neglect.

Experts predict that "the number of compulsive gamblers could soon quadruple from 5 million to 20 million addicts nationwide." The primary reason for this anticipated increase in compulsive gambling is the Internet. With the accessibility of the Internet, gamblers do not have to travel to casinos or contact their local bookie to place a bet. Internet gambling is more addictive than other forms of gambling because it combines high-speed, instant gratification with the anonymity of gambling from home. The temptations that lead to compulsive gambling are as close as one's computer.

Despite the severe impact that pathological gambling has on Americans, minimal research exists on the topic. The research performed on pathological gambling has often been half-hearted. . . .

Compulsive gamblers are responsible for an estimated fifteen percent of the dollars lost in gambling. Beyond this monetary figure, how can society quantify a divorce caused by a gambling addiction or a gambling-induced suicide?. . .

Options to Stop Internet Gambling

After analyzing the statutory landscape of Internet gambling and assessing its negative economic consequences, the question that remains is what can be done to limit Internet gambling? One option is . . . to limit Internet gambling through enhanced enforcement mechanisms against credit card providers and money transfer agents. The Internet gambling industry is dependent on transactions from money transfer agents; thus, discouraging transactions will limit Internet gambling. . . .

Credit Card Use Must Be Limited

An estimated ninety-five percent of Internet gamblers worldwide make their wagers with credit cards. Without question, credit cards are vital to the Internet gambling industry. It would seem logical that limiting the use of credit cards in Internet gambling would decimate the industry. Representative Jim Leach [of Iowa] believes the number of personal bankruptcies will greatly increase if credit card companies continue to allow gamblers to use their products to pay for Internet gambling. Leach introduced a bill in 2001 "that would ban the use of credit cards . . . to pay for Internet gambling." He believed that "the banning of major credit cards may take a thirty percent bite out of the Internet gambling industry in the short run."

One option to impede the use of credit cards and money transfers in Internet gambling would be to enact legislation prohibiting wire transfers to known Internet gambling sites. A problem with this proposal is that with the fluidity of the Internet, alternative forms of payment, such as digital cash, could likely be utilized. Cardholders could easily circumvent the law by buying "electronic cash" at a site such as PayPal. PayPal is described as "an e-commerce provider that allows individuals to establish a PayPal account by depositing funds." Once the account is established, individuals can purchase goods from any site that uses the PayPal system, including Internet gambling sites. Additionally, credit card companies believe a ban on credit card use in Internet gambling transactions would place an unreasonable burden on themselves to enforce federal law. Nonetheless, legislation that hinders an individual's ability to use a credit card for Internet gambling transactions would clearly affect the industry in the near term. At a time when the laws surrounding Internet gambling are ambiguous, any action that would limit the growth of the industry would be beneficial to the economy.

One final possibility would be to enact legislation that made any credit card debt incurred while gambling online unrecoverable. While this type of legislation would not promote consumer responsibility, it would crush the Internet gambling industry. If banks and credit card companies had no avenue to enforce debt collection from Internet gamblers, they would inevitably refuse transactions with Internet gambling sites. . . .

As this [viewpoint] demonstrates, the Internet gambling industry yields a negative impact on the U.S. economy. Internet gambling deprives state and local governments of valuable tax revenues required to maintain services. Internet gambling also forces consumers to pay higher fees and interest rates as a result of uncollectible gambling debts. Finally, Internet gambling adversely affects our society in ways that cannot easily be quantified, such as addiction, pathological behavior, and family disintegration.

In order to limit the negative effects of Internet gambling on our economy, legislators need to take aggressive measures. . . . The negative effects of Internet gambling are already being perceived by the U.S. economy. If lawmakers do not aggressively combat the growth of Internet gambling, the effects on our economy will be damaging.

| "Instead of outlawing [Internet gambling], Congress should regulate it."

Internet Gambling Should Be Regulated, Not Banned

David Carruthers

In the following viewpoint, David Carruthers argues that Internet gambling should be regulated, not banned, in the United States. Carruthers maintains that current laws regarding Internet gambling are hard to enforce, and further legislation seems unwarranted because the public seems in favor of wagering online. He claims that if the U.S. government would only choose to regulate the industry—an industry that will not disappear despite a ban—then the nation could reap revenues and other benefits from a growing, legitimate business. Carruthers was the chief executive officer of BetOnSports, an Internet gambling corporation, at the time the article was written in March 2006. He was arrested in July 2006 on charges of racketeering, conspiracy, and fraud because of his involvement with the betting site.

As you read, consider the following questions:

1. How large, monetarily, is the Internet gambling industry, and how much did it grow between 2001 and 2005, according to Carruthers?

David Carruthers, "Don't Bet Against Online Gambling," *Los Angeles Times*, March 15, 2006. Reproduced by permission of the author.

2. What three concerns about Internet gambling does the author say can be overcome by having the government regulate the industry?

3. In Carruthers's opinion, what does the British Gambling Act provide for the Internet gambling industry and its consumers?

People who never bet on sports make an exception [in March]. Something about the NCAA [National Collegiate Athletic Association] basketball tournament—maybe it's the appeal of filling out those brackets and tracking their progress each day—brings out the gambler in all of us. But if some members of Congress get their way, we won't be able to place any of those bets online.

The proposed Internet Gambling Protection Act would prohibit using the Internet to operate a gaming business. But trying to shut down a multibillion-dollar industry with consumer demand that includes an estimated 8 million Americans annually is an empty legislative effort. Instead of outlawing it, Congress should regulate it.

Online gambling is now a $12-billion-a-year industry. Americans anted up more than $500 million to bet on [the 2006] Super Bowl online, an increase of more than 12% from [2005] and more than five times the amount wagered through Nevada casinos. Overall, Americans wagered nearly $6 billion online in 2005, compared to about $1.5 billion in 2001.

Illegality Is Based on an Outdated Law

The U.S. government says the consumers who placed these bets are in violation of the Wire Act [of 1961] which was originally aimed at organized crime and sought to prevent gambling businesses from operating by phone in states where it was otherwise illegal to gamble.

This law, therefore, shouldn't be applied to Internet betting. Besides, no case law or statute clearly defines where In-

The Need for Global Regulation of Internet Gambling

Evolving technology is increasingly outpacing the ability of individual governments to regulate Internet gambling activity and of law enforcement to enforce such regulations. Therefore, the resolution of these matters must be addressed at the international level. A policy of legalizing, regulating, and licensing Internet gambling operations would provide incentives for the operators to subscribe to the policy standards and investigative requirements set by a universal regulation. The proposed universal regulation includes the creation and implementation of an international regulatory board to issue licenses to operators and monitor conduct on a regular basis. The regulation would additionally provide for restrictions of gambling in certain nations or states explicitly opposed to all forms of gambling, such as Utah and Hawaii. Furthermore, the regulation would ensure a system of equitable tax distribution and would actively monitor and address instances of underage and problem gambling.

Jonathan R. Ehtessabian, Cyberspace Law Seminar, April 16, 2004.

ternet bets are actually taking place. BetOnSports, for example, is based in Costa Rica. Customers can place bets from anywhere that has an Internet connection. In part because of this ambiguity, no one has been prosecuted for online betting under the law.

Enforcing this outdated law, or passing new legislation, would be foolish at best and a violation of privacy and individual freedom at worst. Politicians who seek to prohibit online wagering in order to prevent underage gambling, excessive gambling and corruption could address these goals more effectively through regulation.

The Internet Gambling Industry Wants Regulation

It may surprise our critics to know that we share their concern about gambling abuse. In fact, we have been seeking support from governments to devise systematic ways to protect vulnerable populations. What this industry needs is regulation, not to be pushed even further into the shadows, where organized crime and less reputable people can carve out a niche for themselves.

Regulation can address a number of important concerns about online gambling. First, we can better prevent underage gambling. Most online gambling companies already try to prevent underage gambling. We don't advertise to anyone 18 or under, for example, and we have clear rules on our sites. Regulation could make these practices more enforceable and extend their reach. New technologies can provide regulators with better information, including the ability to provide an audit trail for each transaction or to block participation by certain players or classes of players.

Second, we can better deter compulsive gambling. Currently, companies use software to help their customers keep track of their betting histories. We can also use this software to impose cooling-off periods. With regulation, these practices, too, could become standard in the industry. And third, regulators can ensure transparency and good corporate governance, as they do in most regulated industries.

The British Model

The good news is that Britain provides a model for the U.S. Its Gambling Act, passed [in] spring [2005] provides for the licensing and regulating of online gambling, including the establishment of a national gambling commission to protect consumers, restrict the access of minors and prevent money-laundering and other criminal activity.

It is time for the U.S. government to face the facts: The issue is not whether it is possible to stop online gambling; the issue is how to regulate a business that not only exists but is growing. We have begun the process by working to create an independent advisory council to establish operating standards acceptable to everyone. Not only would regulation strengthen companies that wish to operate responsibly, but legalizing our companies could also bring in billions of dollars in tax revenue. That's one gamble that would generate benefits for all Americans.

> "History has shown us that prohibiting
> private, consensual behavior has never
> made that behavior go away."

Banning Internet Gambling Will Not Stop It

Radley Balko

Radley Balko is a senior editor for Reason *magazine and a former policy analyst for the Cato Institute, a libertarian public policy organization. In the following viewpoint, he argues that banning Internet gambling is a waste of time and that any ban is an erosion of civil liberties. But more significantly, Balko claims that a ban would not deter Americans from wagering on-line. Maintaining the criminality of Internet gambling, he asserts, will only keep the industry from U.S. soil, meaning that gambling providers will be out of the reach of U.S. law and players will thus be unprotected from possible fraud or other illicit gambling scams.*

As you read, consider the following questions:

1. In Balko's view, how have the U.S. government's attempts to prohibit consensual crimes backfired?

Radley Balko, "Anti-Gambling Crusade a Bad Bet," Cato Institute, March 21, 2006. Originally published in the *Arizona Republic*, March 12, 2006. Reproduced by permission of the Cato Institute.

2. In what way is the crusade against Internet gambling hypocritical, according to the author?

3. How does Balko connect organized crime and terrorism to the debate about Internet gambling sites?

Online gambling is already illegal in the United States. Proprietors of gaming sites are all incorporated overseas. Yet Internet wagering is still a $12 billion industry.

History has shown us that prohibiting private, consensual behavior has never made that behavior go away. Because consensual crimes take no victims, vice laws are difficult to enforce: Police have to use informers and undercover work and sometimes need to break the very laws they're trying to enforce.

Consequently, America's various attempts at prohibiting sinful behavior have bred corruption, organized crime, black markets and significant erosion of our civil liberties. The story's no different with gambling. . . .

Gambling Is a Voluntary Choice

What we do with our own money on our own time ought to be our own business. The idea that government is somehow obligated, or even authorized, to protect us from our own vices and "bad" habits simply isn't compatible with a free society.

If five poker enthusiasts want to voluntarily play online, and if a private company wants to provide the technology for that to happen in exchange for a fee, why do members of Congress feel obligated to prevent that from happening?

Like many bad laws, gambling prohibition is often justified in defense of "the children." But for a minor to wager online, he'd need a credit card or access to a bank account. It isn't as if children are easy prey for gambling sites.

A Government Ban on Internet Gambling Is Un-American

Here's the upshot my fellow Americans (and freedom-loving Libertarian Republicans). Prohibition failed miserably the first time around. You cannot tell free men what to do with their own lives and money. Or how to entertain themselves. The fact is—it's none of your business how I choose to entertain myself, or how I choose to spend my money, or what I choose to do in my bedroom, or what I choose to do on my own computer. It is not government's job to try to protect me (or save me). As [President] Ronald Reagan said, "The 9 worst words in the English language are: I'm from the government and I'm here to help.". . .

The government will fail miserably in their attempt to ban online gaming too. The genie is out of the bottle. The train has left the station. You can't stop American men (and a few women too) from doing what they love to do—betting on sports or playing poker online. You can't control our minds. You can't control our computers. You can't control our wallets. There is only one solution—freedom. Legalize online gaming, regulate it, and tax it. Then watch the billions of new tax dollars flow in—money to pay for homeland security education, deficit reduction, and gambling addiction programs. If you ban it—the tax dollars disappear; the gambling addiction problem moves underground and worsens; the profits go to organized crime; and just like during Prohibition—normally law-abiding American citizens lose respect for the law.

Wayne Allyn Root, Gambling911.com, September 30, 2006.

Gambling Legislation Is Hypocritical

[In February 2006] police in Fairfax, Va., conducted a SWAT raid on Sal Culosi Jr., an optometrist suspected of running a sports gambling pool with some friends. As the SWAT team surrounded him, one officer's gun discharged, struck Culosi in the chest and killed him. In the fiscal year before the raid that killed Culosi, Virginia spent about $20 million marketing and promoting its state lottery.

The scene is similar in other states. Charity and barroom poker games, for example, are being shut down by police departments across the country. Meanwhile, state lotteries are cashing in on the poker craze with Texas Hold'em-style scratch-off games.

Congress isn't immune from the double standard. The anti-gambling bill sponsored by Virginia Rep. Bob Goodlatte contains a gaping loophole that lets state lotteries continue to sell their tickets online. And just as Goodlatte, Arizona Sen. Jon Kyl and others in Congress have been earnestly lecturing us on why we need our politicians to protect us from our own peccadilloes, 28 states, including Arizona, were cashing in on the hyped $365 million Powerball jackpot.

Which makes all these efforts to ban private gambling sound more like a protection racket than good government.

Banning Internet Gambling Will Not Work

As noted, despite prohibitions against Internet gambling, it's still a billion-dollar industry. Prohibitionists have argued that a law preventing credit-card companies from allowing their services to be used in conjunction with gaming sites will prove to be the death knell for online wagering.

Hardly. In fact, several state attorneys general already have gone after the credit companies and online payment services like PayPal, threatening them with Patriot Act charges for doing business with gaming sites. Consequently, third-party vendors such as Neteller, also located offshore, have sprung up to facilitate transactions between gamers and gaming sites.

Congress can keep passing laws. But so long as there is demand, innovators will continue to use technology to find ways around them.

On CNBC [in 2006], Goodlatte pointed out that because gambling companies themselves are offshore, they aren't subject to U.S. laws and regulations. But that's an argument against his own bill. Goodlatte's bill won't stop Internet gaming. Instead, it will not only keep gaming companies offshore, it will facilitate the rise of offshore financing services, too.

That means U.S. consumers will be more susceptible to fraud and will have no legal recourse when a shady offshore outfit bilks them out of their money.

Not to mention that offshore, black-market outfits present prime funding opportunities for organized crime and international terrorism.

A more sensible policy would be to legalize online gambling and let credible gaming companies do business within the reach of U.S. law. The good ones are already begging to be regulated.

They understand that legitimately setting up shop in the United States will give them an advantage over their competitors. Consumers will be more likely to place bets on sites governed by U.S. laws and subject to U.S. courts.

Unfortunately, Congress seems more interested in pushing a moral agenda than taking a realistic approach to a habit that is as old as human nature.

| "Half the proposals these days to curb gambling are really about protecting a gambling monopoly."

A Government Ban on Internet Gambling Is Hypocritical

Froma Harrop

In the following viewpoint, Froma Harrop argues that the U.S. government holds a monopoly on gambling and that much of the legislation to prohibit gambling—including Internet gambling—is created only to strengthen this monopoly. She states that she has opposed the spread of legalized gambling in the past, but concedes that if one form of gambling is legal, then all forms should be legal. Harrop is a syndicated columnist and a member of the editorial board of the Providence Journal *in Rhode Island.*

As you read, consider the following questions:

1. Where is sports betting legal in the United States, according to the author?

2. What hypocrisy exists within the Internet Gambling Prohibition Act, according to Harrop?

3. In the author's view, what are the two "good things" about online gambling?

The FBI is shocked, SHOCKED that Americans will illegally bet an estimated $2.4 billion on March Madness college basketball [the National Collegiate Athletic Association (NCAA) basketball tournament]. Perhaps they'll round up the usual suspects—all several million of them.

Gambling Ban Is Immoral

You see, gambling is immoral, except when done through lotteries, keno, off-track betting, Indian casinos, riverboat casinos, dog races, horse races, jai-alai frontons, card rooms and other wagering venues blessed by the states. And betting on college sports is especially evil, unless you do it in Las Vegas, whose casinos expect to make about $90 million off March Madness alone.

I have long opposed the proliferation of gambling, but the time's come to give up. Let the state-approved slot machines multiply—but also the online gambling sites, most of which happen to be (who cares anymore?) illegal.

The monopoly of gambling has become more immoral than the activity itself. Wherever a politician can deliver the right to virtually print money, corruption breeds. The most colorful example is lobbyist-crook Jack Abramoff, who made millions defrauding the [Native American] tribes that hired him to guard their casino monopolies.

Bans on Gambling Protect Monopolies

It's against the law to bet on sporting events, with Nevada the grandfathered exception. Casinos in other states want a piece of the action, but Nevada has opposed changing the law, for obvious reasons. And efforts to simply outlaw gambling on college games have failed, again with Nevada leading the opposition.

The NCAA basketball tournament is second only to the Super Bowl as the biggest sports-gambling event. An estimated $4 billion in wagers will be made during March Madness, with online betting sites expected to scoop up a third of the total. That can't be good news either for the state-approved gambling ventures or the underworld ones. Internet gambling, most of it run from overseas, is still in its infancy. And it is as unstoppable as it is illegal.

Not that Washington hasn't tried to stifle the online competition. The U.S. Justice Department, for example, ordered American radio and television stations not to run ads for Internet gambling sites. But Antigua dragged the United States before the World Trade Organization [WTO] over the matter [in 2004]. The Caribbean nation, home to many of the Websites, argued that the United States was violating free-trade agreements to protect the industry at home. The WTO agreed with Antigua.

Congress is considering the Internet Gambling Prohibition Act [in 2006]. It would stop banks and credit card companies from processing transactions with overseas betting sites. One of the sponsors, Arizona Sen. Jon Kyl, produced a report [in 2003] explaining why a similar bill was necessary—basically, to protect the social fabric.

Internet betting "encourages youth gambling," Kyl wrote, and "exacerbates pathological gambling." The report ended with a cymbal crash of hypocrisy: the legislation, Kyl noted, "contains language to ensure the continuation of currently lawful Internet gambling by the Indian tribes." It comes as no surprise that the latest version does the same.

A Threat to Honest Government

Either we let Americans gamble legally or we don't. The growth of gambling outlets has indeed led to a rise in bankruptcy, suicide, robbery, embezzlement, divorce and other social ills. And state governments fool no one when they fund counseling organizations for people brought low by gambling activities that the states themselves raise revenues from.

But there seems little point in having a Connecticut Council on Problem Gambling when Connecticut has no problem hosting [the tribal casino] Foxwoods, the biggest slot-machine emporium in the United States, another major casino nearby and a state lottery. Let it be noted that half the people who call the council's hotline have annual incomes of less than $35,000. (Foxwoods now wants to open a slots operation on Philadelphia's riverfront.)

While the proliferation of gambling hurts the weakest members of society, its biggest threat right now is to honest government. Thus, there are two good things about online gambling: One is that it cannibalizes the government-created monopolies. The other is it's not in everyone's face. The office betting pool, though also illegal, shares the merit of leaving politicians out of the transaction.

March Madness [is] over in a few days, but the mad rush to carve out exclusive rights to milk the public is year-round. And remember: Half the proposals these days to curb gambling are really about protecting a gambling monopoly.

Periodical Bibliography

The following articles have been selected to supplement the diverse views presented in this chapter.

Frank Catania	"Congress Shouldn't Throttle Internet Gambling," *Hill*, September 27, 2006.
Economist	"Texas Hold'em: Online Gambling," July 22, 2006.
Camden R. Fine	"ICBA Tells Senate Gambling Legislation Bill (HR 4411) Would Create Impossible Compliance Burden," *Online Wire*, August 4, 2006. www.theonlinewire.com.
Peter Gumbel	"How the U.S. Is Getting Beat in Online Gambling," *Time*, November 28, 2005.
Robert Hahn and Paul Tetlock	"Short Odds for Ignorance," *New York Times*, October 12, 2006.
Douglas Muir	"Congress Puts a Chokehold on Virtual Casinos for Good Reason," *Portland Press Herald/ Maine Sunday Telegram*, October 15, 2006.
Matthew Norman	"Only the U.S. Could Ban Online Gambling," *Independent* (London), October 6, 2006.
Emma Schwartz	"Crux of Case: Is Online Gambling Legal?" *Fulton County* (Georgia) *Daily Report*, August 29, 2006.
James Surowiecki	"Wages of Sin," *New Yorker*, September 25, 2006.
Aaron Todd	"Internet Poker Needs Federal, Not State Solution," *Casino City Times*, June 21, 2006. www.casinocitytimes.com.
Jacob Weisbert	"Don't Bet on It: The Silly War on Internet Gambling," *Slate*, July 26, 2006. www.slate.com.
George F. Will	"Prohibition II: Good Grief," *Newsweek*, October 23, 2006.

OPPOSING VIEWPOINTS® SERIES

CHAPTER 3

Is Compulsive Gambling a Problem?

Chapter Preface

Since 1980 the American Psychiatric Association (APA) has recognized problem gambling as an impulse control disorder in which the individual is compelled to repeatedly perform an act regardless of the potential for harm. The APA's *Diagnostic and Statistical Manual for Mental Disorders* (*DSM-III* and *DSM-IV*) categorizes problem or pathological gambling as a mental disorder that should be treated as such. While this has been the clinical assessment of problem gambling, many people still consider problem gambling the result of personal weakness or lack of moral strength to resist temptation.

Members of the psychiatric community, however, are attempting to better treat pathological gambling by seeing in it qualities that link it closely to alcoholism and drug addiction. Following this line of thinking, recent studies have claimed that neurological drugs could be used for the treatment of problem gambling. The *American Journal of Psychiatry* (*AJP*) published a clinical study in its February 2006 issue that examines the use of nalmefene, a drug that inhibits certain neurochemicals in the brain that are linked with increased rates of addictive behavior, to curb pathological gambling behaviors. Results of the study suggest that using this treatment, previously used on individuals suffering from drug and alcohol addiction, has the potential to produce the same positive results for pathological gamblers.

Robert Freedman, MD, the editor-in-chief of the *AJP*, confirms that the aims of the test are not only to find treatment, but also to remove the stigma associated with problem gambling. He states, "The study is part of emerging evidence that gambling, once thought to be a problem with moral integrity, is instead a problem in brain biology and can be treated successfully." In addition, by referring to this disorder as pathological gambling instead of the more common and suggestive term *compulsive gambling*, the APA has attempted to deemphasize the moral issues associated with the problem and to highlight the disorder's biological roots.

Whether it is called by its clinical name or the more commonplace term, problem gambling still affects the lives of thousands of Americans. The authors presented in the following chapter offer a range of viewpoints debating the gravity of pathological gambling's impact on society and the role legalized gambling may be playing in promoting the disorder.

❚ *"Out-of-control gambling is on the rise."*

Compulsive Gambling Is a Serious Problem

Harvard Mental Health Letter

In the following viewpoint, the Harvard Mental Health Letter *argues that because of the prevalence of casino and Internet gambling in the United States, more players are showing signs of problem gambling (also called compulsive or pathological gambling). As a result of this disorder, problem gamblers are injuring family relationships, jeopardizing careers, and sometimes embracing criminal activities to pay off gambling debts. Treatment for problem gamblers, the letter notes, is an inexact science; therefore, the nation should address compulsive gambling as a social problem if it is to be curbed.*

As you read, consider the following questions:

1. What are some of the illegal activities problem gamblers might engage in, according to the author?
2. As the author reports, how does the American Psychiatric Association classify pathological gambling?
3. According to the author, what problems do treatment programs—such as Gamblers Anonymous—experience?

Adapted from *Harvard Mental Health Letter*, "Problem Gambling," vol. 20, no. 9, March 2004. www.health.harvard.edu/newsweek/Problem_gambling.htm. Republished with permission of Harvard Health Publications.

Gambling has become increasingly legitimate and socially acceptable. Most states have legalized it in some form, and it's one of the nation's fastest-growing industries, already attracting more customers than baseball or movies. Credit requirements have been relaxed and facilities are more accessible. Gambling expenditures have more than doubled since 1975. One in two adults bought a lottery ticket and nearly a third visited a casino during the last year. States depend on lotteries to fill their treasuries, and casinos are the main source of income on some Native American reservations. Technological advances continually supply easier and more enticing ways to play; the latest is the Internet. Inevitably, out-of-control gambling is on the rise. It's now recognized as a psychiatric disorder and a challenge for mental health treatment.

Compulsive gamblers are constantly thinking about past bets, planning the next one, and finding the money to support the habit. They increase the size of their wagers and struggle to quit or cut back. Unable to tolerate losing, they immediately try to recoup. They gamble when they are disappointed or frustrated; neglect their families; lose jobs, careers, and marriages to the habit; sell personal property, borrow, beg, lie, steal, and write bad checks to finance gambling or pay their debts. Often they are repeatedly bailed out by their families. The American Insurance Institute has called gambling the main cause of white-collar crime.

According to the National Council on Problem Gambling, about 1% of American adults—nearly 3 million people—are pathological gamblers. Another 2%–3% have less serious but still significant problems, and as many as 15 million are at risk, with at least two of the symptoms described by the American Psychiatric Association.

Most compulsive gamblers are men, but the problem is growing among women. African Americans have a higher rate of compulsive gambling than whites, and the rate is about twice the average among those living within 50 miles of a ca-

Definition of Pathological Gambling

Pathological gambling involves five or more of the following:

- Preoccupation with past, present, and future gambling experiences and with ways to obtain money for gambling.

- Need to increase the amount of wagers.

- Repeated unsuccessful efforts to cut back or stop.

- Becoming restless or irritable when trying to cut back or stop.

- Gambling to escape from everyday problems or to relieve feelings of helplessness, anxiety, or depression.

- Trying to recoup immediately after losing money (chasing losses).

- Lying about gambling.

- Committing illegal acts to finance gambling.

- Losing or jeopardizing a personal relationship, job, or career opportunity because of gambling.

- Requesting gifts or loans to pay gambling debts.

Adapted from the American Psychiatric Association's
Diagnostic and Statistical Manual of Mental Disorders IV, *1994.*

sino. The poor and people with limited education, exposed to tempting visions of unattainable wealth, are particularly susceptible.

Experts often distinguish gambling for action from gambling to escape. Action gamblers, highly competitive and easily bored, tend to take unnecessary risks and make impulsive decisions. They often prefer poker and blackjack, horse races, professional and college sports, and stock market speculation—where they can exercise some skill, or at least the appearance of skill. Escape gamblers are more likely to play passive games of pure chance—slot machines, bingo, and lotteries. They are often depressed or anxious and use gambling to numb or cheer themselves.

A biological predisposition could be involved. Twin studies indicate that heredity may account for up to 35% of individual differences in susceptibility to gambling problems. Some research suggests that pathological gamblers have abnormal activity in areas of the frontal lobes that are centers of judgment and decision-making. But gambling problems cannot be reduced to genetics or neurochemistry. Biological research is still scarce, and the results have to be corrected for the presence of other psychiatric disorders.

Such disorders are common. Compulsive gamblers have high rates of depression, mania, alcohol and drug abuse, and some personality disorders. In a survey of Gamblers Anonymous members, 22% reported panic attacks, 72% reported an episode of major depression, and 52% reported alcohol abuse. As in all such situations, it's difficult to distinguish between causes and effects. The results of irrational betting while intoxicated lead to more drinking. Gambling losses cause depression, which leads to more gambling. Eventually, whatever the origin of the problem, the pattern becomes self-perpetuating.

It's a pattern typical of addiction, and that's how most experts now regard pathological gambling. Although the American Psychiatric Association formally classifies it as an impulse control disorder, the description closely parallels alcoholism and drug dependence. The thrill of the wager corresponds to intoxication. Increasing the size of bets corresponds to tolerance and taking more than intended. The restlessness and irritability of abstaining gamblers are a kind of withdrawal reaction. The bailout—a loan or gift to pay debts in return for a promise to quit—corresponds to detoxification without further treatment. The origin of the word "addict" fits this picture; it's an ancient Roman term referring to persons legally enslaved for defaulting on debts.

The treatment of compulsive gambling also resembles substance abuse treatment. Widely used methods include psychodynamic therapy, 12-step groups, motivational interviewing, and cognitive-behavioral therapies, often in combination. . . .

Although some treatment is almost certainly better than none, little is known about which treatments work best for which gamblers. There are few randomized controlled trials. Behavioral and cognitive therapies, which have been studied most carefully, seem to be effective for some, at least in the short run. One study found that motivational interviewing plus a mailed self-help workbook was more effective than the workbook alone or assignment to a waiting list. The advantage persisted for six months, but no longer.

Gamblers Anonymous, like Alcoholics Anonymous, has undoubtedly transformed some lives, but the dropout rate is high, and it's not clear how much the confessional meetings help the general run of people with gambling problems. In one study, only 8% of members had achieved abstinence for a year or more. Besides, many gamblers want to return to controlled betting instead of the abstinence required by Gamblers Anonymous principles.

The 1999 National Gambling Impact Study Commission report recommends more research on how to encourage compulsive gamblers to seek treatment and how to help their families. The Commission also calls for more study of the connections between gambling, mood disorders, and alcoholism; the effects of gambling on bankruptcy, suicide, divorce, and crime rates; and the new problems created by electronic and Internet gambling.

Like alcoholism and drug addiction, pathological gambling is a social problem that demands more than individual therapeutic solutions.

| "Compulsive gambling is an overrated problem."

The Problem of Compulsive Gambling Is Exaggerated

Dan Seligman

In the following viewpoint, Dan Seligman argues that the problem of compulsive gambling is exaggerated by gambling's detractors. In Seligman's view, most Americans enjoy gambling and have no ill effects from this harmless entertainment. Seligman suggests that those who have problems controlling their gambling may be suffering from other issues—such as alcoholism or drug addiction—that simply manifest as a compulsion to gamble. Seligman, long a respected journalist at Time, Inc., now writes for Forbes.

As you read, consider the following questions:

1. As Seligman explains it, what is the principle of diminishing marginal utility?
2. According to the National Academy of Sciences report cited by the author, what percentage of the adult population is composed of problem gamblers?

3. What is "co-morbidity" and how does Seligman relate it to the issue of problem gambling?

Compulsive gambling is an overrated problem, and the latest research on gamblers suggests we need to rethink it.

A curious thing about gambling in America is that it is extremely popular, yet has a bad reputation—and I don't mean the unsavory way in which gambling licenses are awarded. . . . I am talking about the moral realm, as witnessed in the clucking over William Bennett's expensive habit.[1] Casinoland's high rollers are perceived as inhabiting a zone somewhere between immoral and diseased, and have great difficulty defending themselves. Yet in their own lives most Americans demand ever more gambling opportunities. As things stand now [in June 2003], legal gambling is available in all but three states (Hawaii, Tennessee and Utah) [it is now legal in Tennessee], and most Americans admit to gambling sometimes. Surveys done in 1999 for the National Gambling Impact Study Commission told us that 86% of Americans had gambled at some time in their lives, and 68% had gambled within the prior year. Total legal wagering runs around $900 billion a year (about 10% of personal income), of which some $600 billion takes place at casinos. Casinos, long confined to Nevada and New Jersey, now also exist in 27 other states (in 15 of which the business is open only to Indians).

That $900 billion covers a broad range of activities, including lotteries, jai alai [a Spanish ball game], pari-mutuel [pooled] betting on horses and dogs, church and secular bingo, sports betting and more—yet it clearly understates the gambling total. It doesn't include illegal betting, whose total is enormous but unknowable. And it doesn't include the gambling done in America's securities markets by day traders and

---

1. Bennett is a political spokesman and public moralist who served in the administrations of Presidents Ronald Reagan and George H.W. Bush. His image as a scourge of public vices, however, was tarnished in 2003 when his penchant for gambling became a media topic.

others. Your broker can perhaps testify to running into customers whose idea of investment is indistinguishable from Las Vegas action. In any event Wall Street offers plenty of bets with risk/reward opportunities that mirror those of slot machines—a long shot with the occasional huge payout. Buying out-of-the-money puts [the option to sell stock at less than current market value] on an airline stock just before a union vote would fall in that category. If the members unexpectedly vote against wage concessions, you could make a killing on the bankruptcy.

Gambling's Evil Image

Despite gambling's broad popularity, its enemies keep coming at it from all directions. To begin with its least influential bad-mouthers, it is generally disfavored by economists. As postulated in several editions of [Harvard professor] Paul Samuelson's famous textbook [of the 1940s, *Foundations of Economic Analysis*], gambling is a bad thing under the principle of diminishing marginal utility. The principle tells us that the $1,000 won on a 999-to-1 bet can buy something less than 1,000 times as much happiness as the dollar put up for the bet. Thus gamblers are collectively losers, even in the idealized lottery, where nothing is taken off the top for overhead and taxes. And, of course, the real world is far from the Platonic ideal—much is lost to overhead.

The other economic formulation has gambling as an evil because it consumes time and resources without creating any new output. You could say the same about climbing Mt. Everest, but somehow economists never weigh in on this front.

What you absolutely never hear from them is that gambling is terrific entertainment, and that perfectly rational people play the lottery and the horses because they get kicks at a price they find reasonable. The price, of course, is not the amount bet but the amount lost by customers succumbing to the vigorish [a charge taken on bets]—the house's edge.

Overestimation Masks the Problem of Compulsive Gambling

Gambling's critics tend to grossly overstate the number of compulsive gamblers. The most recent (impartial) estimate is that approximately 1 percent of the U.S. adult population are pathological gamblers (source: NORC [National Opinion Research Center]). In [a] 1999 report, the NGISC [National Gambling Impact Study Commission] reported this figure to be about 0.9 percent. Furthermore, a 1997 study by Harvard Medical School's Division on Addictions estimated the number slightly higher—at 1.29 percent. The Harvard report was a comprehensive analysis of 120 previously conducted independent studies on problem gambling disorders. Based on the three studies, there appears to be a general consensus that approximately 1 percent (or about three million people) of the U.S. adult population can be classified as pathological gamblers. While a serious issue, this is far less than the numbers afflicted with other compulsive disorders, such as drug abuse and alcoholism. This is also a far cry from the numbers alleged by opponents of gambling, which have estimated that as many as 15 percent of gamblers have a compulsive disorder.

Nolan Dalla, Card Player, *August 17, 2001.*

You also don't hear this being acknowledged by people whose livelihood comes from fighting compulsive gambling and who are, therefore, somewhat motivated to exaggerate the problem's magnitude. Gamblers Anonymous, the National Council on Problem Gambling (and its state affiliates), the Compulsive Gambling Center, the International Centre for Youth Gambling Problems, the Chinese Community Problem Gambling Project, Women Helping Women (publishers of a female gambling recovery newsletter) and the Association of

Problem Gambling Service Administrators are all out there getting across the message that compulsive gambling is ruining lives. In an average month the Nexis database adds 200 articles mentioning "problem" gambling and 100 or so mentioning "compulsive" gambling.

Everything Has Risk

Yet the overwhelming majority of gamblers are just out there enjoying themselves. The best available—though still flawed—research on the numbers is the study performed several years ago by a panel of the National Academy of Sciences (NAS), which indicated that compulsive gamblers are about 0.9% of the adult population. There is no longer any dispute about the characters in question being seriously self-destructive, as we were reminded recently by the April [2003] obituary of Leonard Tose, who was forced to sell the Philadelphia Eagles to pay $25 million in casino gambling debts. (Charming detail from the *New York Times* obit: It was Lenny's habit to take over blackjack tables and repetitively play seven games simultaneously, at $10,000 apiece.) The NAS says another 2% or so are "problem" gamblers, but this figure is suspect if only because the accompanying definition is so wobbly. A problem gambler is said to be a guy (about two-thirds are male) whose betting "results in any harmful effects" to himself or folks around him. Any harmful effects? Everything you do, from driving cars to taking showers, has some potential for harmful effects.

Possibly you are telling yourself that characters like Leonard Tose do so much damage, to themselves and others, that we must do everything possible to curb the disease, even if its victims are relatively few. It is not clear, however, that we know how to deal with the disease. The National Council on Problem Gambling, one of many organizations that "certifies" counselors to treat problem gamblers, acknowledges that among those who seek counseling, 75% drop out of the programs they are steered to, and only half of the remainder end up abstaining from gambling—an overall success rate of about one-eighth, and this in a group presumed (because they came in voluntarily) to be above average in their motivation.

Perhaps Gambling Is Not the Problem

But the success rate is not the main issue. Recent psychiatric research into compulsive gambling gets into "co-morbidity"— that is, the tendency of problem gamblers to have problems that go beyond gambling. It turns out that alcoholism and drug addiction are rampant among problem gamblers (Tose was an alcoholic), and the NAS study indicates that they also have high rates of depression, schizophrenia and "antisocial personality disorder" some three times higher than the rates among nongamblers. All of which raises an interesting question: Is there any such thing as problem gamblers who are otherwise normal? I recently asked this question of Christine Reilly, executive director of the Harvard Medical School's Institute for Pathological Gambling, and she said: "If there is such a group, it's probably a very small group."

Next question: Is it possible that among pathological gamblers, the gambling itself is not really the problem, or at least not the ultimate problem—that it's simply the expression of those other "morbidities"? There are hints in the NAS study that some researchers are close to answering yes to that question, e.g., in a passage indicating drug and alcohol problems are associated with "progression to problem gambling and pathological gambling." And if the answer is affirmative, it would seem to follow that we wouldn't really get very far by limiting gambling opportunities. There are, after all, plenty of other ways for drunks and drug addicts to ruin their own and their families' lives.

| *"The evidence suggests that youth gambling addiction is becoming a real social problem in America."*

Compulsive Gambling Is a Growing Problem Among Teenagers

Mark Alden and James Silver

In the following viewpoint, Mark Alden and James Silver argue that teenagers are using the Internet to play poker for money. Although the authors state that underage gambling is illegal, they note that teenagers find it easy and anonymous to wager through online casinos. With such access, many teens are becoming addicted to online poker and consequently losing large sums of money, Alden and Silver contend. Alden is a producer for Britain's BBC radio. Silver is a reporter for the BBC and has written for many British print news sources.

As you read, consider the following questions:

1. What do the authors say is the only identification needed to register at Partypoker.com?

2. In Alden and Silver's view, why is it difficult to gauge the number of teenagers gambling on the Internet?

3. Why has the U.S. government resisted prosecuting illegal gambling online, in the authors' opinion?

One of the most common ways for young players, those under the legal age for gambling, to get a taste for poker is by gambling on the plethora of free, gambling-for-fun [Web] sites. Many of the biggest online companies run these sites side-by-side with their "for money" sites. Critics, however, say the fun sites act as a kind of gamblers' nursery school, teaching young novices the rules of the game, while often whetting the appetite by bombarding them with pop-ups urging them to play for hard cash.

Richard Segal of Party Gaming stresses that they do everything they can to stop underage gamblers from logging on to the real money sites.

"We are very, very clear that we do not want people unless they are of suitable age to play on our sites," says Segal, "and we take, as an organization, responsible gaming very, very seriously. When it comes to depositing money, as an individual, you need to give us information about yourself, about your age, and in terms of making payments, about the form of payment that you're going to make. I would like to believe that as a responsible operator, we pick up the vast majority of underage players. You know it would be foolish of me to say it is 100 percent fool-proof, but we try and be as good as we possibly can."

Easy Access to Online Gambling

We decided to see for ourselves what actually happens when you register at Partypoker.com. There certainly didn't appear to be too many visible security systems in place to us. As far as we could see, all you need is access to an adult's credit card details with the correct billing address and be prepared to enter a false date of birth, and you're good to go.

That's not the case in some other countries. In the United Kingdom, for example, those registering on Party Poker's site today [in 2006] are also asked to supply a passport or driver's license number. That data is then cross-referenced with the credit card details supplied.

But here in America, home to over half of the world's online gamblers, the adolescents we spoke to described gaining access to several of the major poker sites as "easy."

A 17-year-old we'll call Paul was one such teen gambler.

"I started playing cards with my friends about two years ago. It was a lot of fun. And I eventually moved up to playing online," Paul recalls. "I played poker mostly, on a number of sites including Party Poker and Paradise Poker. I found that was fun too. So I began betting money there. I had no difficulty whatsoever in playing for money online with cards. You know, I used friends' credit cards and other methods—bank accounts, debit cards, credit cards—and overall I probably lost $5–6,000 this way."

Despite the fact that he was 16 years old and losing thousands of dollars, Paul says that neither he, nor any of the owners of the credit cards he was using, were ever questioned about his age.

"There was no real age verification and there was no proof of anything needed. Basically anyone at all can play poker online. I would just play for hours at a time online and I was betting too much and I really was not in control of my gambling and it became a problem, and I'm now in Gamblers Anonymous here in New Jersey."

Youth Gambling Addiction Is on the Rise

It's pretty much impossible to know accurately how many underage gamblers there are out there, mainly because they're logging on with false identities. But the national helpline, 1-800-Gambler, told us that the number of adolescents calling them for help has doubled [since 2003].

The Gambling Problem on College Campuses

According to the National Council on Problem Gambling, 85 percent of the adult population has gambled at least once. A national study done this past summer [2005] by the Annenberg Public Policy Center at the University of Pennsylvania established that more than half of all college students surveyed admitted to gambling at least once a month.

A Harvard study found that 4.67 percent of young people have a gambling problem, citing that 42 percent of college students surveyed said they gamble primarily to make money.

Recent research has also shown that college students are more likely to develop a gambling addiction. Pathological gambling, as it is sometimes called, occurs in 1 to 2 percent of the adult population in the United States, while the rates climb to 4 to 8 percent for college students.

Vincent Gesuele, October 5, 2005. www.statehornet.com.

The evidence suggests that youth gambling addiction is becoming a real social problem in America. Technically, Internet gambling, like any other form of telephone betting, is, in fact, illegal under the 1961 Wire Act. But David Schwartz, director at the Center for Gaming Research at the University of Nevada, Las Vegas, says the law, and its interpretation, are complex.

"The Wire Act was passed in 1961 and it was done at the behest of Attorney General Robert F. Kennedy who wanted to crack down on organized crime," Schwartz says. "According to the letter of the law, anyone who was involved in placing or helping the placing of bets is guilty of a crime, can be sent to prison and fined for that."

But Schwartz says the spirit of the 1961 law is a different matter.

"Robert Kennedy gave it deliberately broad scope so bookmakers couldn't say, 'We're not really running a business, just accepting bets from friends.' But the Wire Act was never intended to be used to prosecute individual bettors, just people who were profiting off of large-scale gambling operations."

Successive administrations have made it clear they won't prosecute any individuals placing bets over the Internet. Hence some 20 million Americans freely gamble online. But the Internet companies are banned from operating on American soil. Nevertheless, to date, there's been little public debate or apparent concern about the proliferation of gambling sites available to American citizens. David Schwartz says there are many cultural reasons for this.

"The United States has traditionally given its citizens, and its citizens have demanded, a great amount of privacy and a great amount of freedom and choice and consumer choice about how they spend their money," Schwartz says. "Many Americans feel what they do on the Internet is their own business. And in order to police the Internet and to prevent people from betting online, you'd have to have someone monitoring every computer in the United States, making sure people aren't going to sites they aren't supposed to. There's been a great outcry against phone-tapping domestically with the 'war on terror' and I can't imagine people would accept government watching their Internet use of gambling which most people think is a harmless diversion."

Part of American Culture

David Schwartz also says gambling has a unique place in American history and culture, which explains why Internet poker has been allowed to flourish here, unchecked.

"Gambling has always been a part of U.S. culture," says Schwartz.

"Gambling's part of our history. Early colonies were financed in part by lotteries. Presidents have gambled. Gambling is a huge part of U.S. life. Poker is a U.S.-exported game. Recently, with television coverage of the World Series of Poker, it's become mainstream. It's become an inextricable part of American culture."

Today, a generation of Americans is growing up on a steady diet of poker. The cards are being dealt 24/7 at home, in school, on television and online. At any given moment, thousands of adolescents are logged in and losing money. The lack of political will to regulate gambling, and the lack of awareness about its hidden dangers, means that America faces a vast, uncontrolled social experiment. Many young poker players will carry a pathological need to gamble into adulthood. So we won't know the full social cost of the Internet poker craze until this generation grows up and has real responsibilities—homes, jobs, children—and much more to lose.

"If the parents aren't involved in the anti-teen gambling movement, then perhaps it's just a smokescreen?"

Teenage Gambling Has Generated Undue Backlash

Maryann Guberman

Maryann Guberman is a writer and editor for many gaming publications. In the following viewpoint, Guberman argues that the backlash against poker in the United States has been motivated in large part by fears of exacerbating teenage gambling. As Guberman points out, though, many parents are unconcerned that their kids are engaging in gaming and view it as a relatively harmless pursuit. This has led her to conclude that the backlash is driven by antigambling interest groups that may be exaggerating the problem.

As you read, consider the following questions:

1. Why does Guberman say that parents are not worried about their children's gambling pursuits?
2. What other "dangerous" teenage crazes does the author say have not experienced a media backlash?

3. What is at the root of the antigambling backlash, according to Guberman?

> Money is the opposite of the weather. Nobody talks about it, but everybody does something about it. —Rebecca Johnson

It was bound to happen. In fact, I think I participated to a degree.

The poker backlash was inevitable. It had to become a mainstream topic.

Just mention poker in the same breath with teenagers and you have an automatic hit.

Where it starts is probably a secret. Maybe it was a masterfully constructed government plan to use a backdoor method to wipe out online gambling; maybe it was some genius marketing agent who was interested in selling his client's compulsive gambling books; maybe it was a well-meaning religious organization, a recovering compulsive or just a well-meaning person who sparked the little flame that's about to turn into a conflagration.

It likely was not Mr. and Mrs. Nobody Public but we'll never know.

Media Attention on Teen Gambling

In June [2005], Court TV carried a special on teenage gambling. Hosted by Al Roker, the program interviewed teens at a Connecticut high school for their opinions about and experiences with gambling. Perhaps not by coincidence, this is the same state where the Connecticut Council on Problem Gambling conducted a survey of almost 4,000 students in five local high schools in 1996 showing that 87 percent of teens gambled on something at sometime (32 percent on the lottery).

The initial study in Connecticut took place before the widespread proliferation of online casinos and definitely before poker became the great American game. Back then, kids

"When you've finished playing
with the children!"

© CartoonStock.com

gambled on sports, lottery, and sometimes, if they could sneak in and get away with it, at casino gambling.

And if you don't think teen gambling is a hot topic, just Google it. Or go to your local library and pick up a copy of *Family Circle*, that magazine about baking perfect cakes and losing perfect weight, and take note of the early January [2005] issue that featured not-so-perfect teen gambling as a cover story.

Just Who Is Concerned?

What's interestingly different now is that as far as most people can ascertain, parents don't see anything wrong with their sons (and daughters, I suppose) playing poker with friends and/or with strangers online. Unlike alcohol and drug addictions and teenage sex, the consequences of gambling don't seem at all negative.

No, it's not mom and dad worried about it. They seem to be okay as long as they know where their kids are and what they're doing. The big worriers are the people who study compulsive gambling, people like the execs at the National Council on Problem Gambling, who flatly state that gambling is outdistancing drugs, drinking and smoking as a high-risk activity.

It might be the money; it could be the let-me-crush-you attitude; it is often the overall challenge that requires very little physical stamina but kids really do seem to enjoy gambling on something more than Monopoly today.

And if their parents don't mind, what's the purpose of this backlash?

I don't know if I really trust the accuracy of the studies cited, especially because there aren't that many groups doing them. After all, I recall surveys being done way back in the sixties when my fellow students bragged about how they lied without hesitation in their responses just to mess up the survey.

Now, quite frankly, having witnessed the personal devastation of compulsive gambling among a small group of people I've known—none of whom were poker players—I realize this can be a severely emotional, devastating problem, especially since the bottom line (money) is the same reason for so many other emotional[ly] devastating problems. I've argued with friends and relatives against the spread of casino gambling to so many American entities.

But if the parents aren't involved in the anti–teen gambling movement, then perhaps it's just a smokescreen?

I've never seen any kind of backlash about other hot new crazes. NASCAR, freestyle snowboarding, BMX motocross stuff never seemed to raise a single eyebrow let alone a massive public relations campaign, and some of those things are deadly!

It Is About the Money

And that's where the backlash probably has to be researched— not from the physical danger (since there isn't any significant physical danger) and perhaps not from the emotional danger (even though there is a potential for severe danger here) because it starts with being all about the money. Teens have difficulty understanding long term. In the midst of their angst, their growing pains, their need to be like their friends, they can't see what lies further ahead than the weekend.

If you view gambling of any kind as a vice, then the poker backlash is a good thing altogether. If you view gambling as an acceptable vice for adults, then it's a good idea to make sure any teens in your family are well-informed.

In truth, by allowing children to gamble (and by children, we're referring to whatever age is used to mark the difference between a child and an adult) we're obscuring the value of money, the value of earning it, the value of using it, the value of saving it, and the value of enjoying it. They haven't learned what money's all about yet.

Donald Trump and other self-styled gamblers like to say it's not the money that counts, it's the action; it's the ability to get the best of your opponent that makes gambling (poker) so great. ("Money was never a big motivation for me, except as a way to keep score. The real excitement is playing the game.")

That's the attitude that could be causing the gambling and poker backlash. No matter what anybody says, it's about the money. Understanding that makes understanding the backlash easy. It's not going to go away but in the long run, unless it hits home after home after home, it's probably not going to impact poker at all.

> "Gambling addiction stories are as common in Nevada as tornado tales are in Kansas."

Casinos Foster Compulsive Gambling

Steve Friess

Steve Friess reports in the following viewpoint that Nevada is home to an inordinate number of compulsive gamblers. In Friess's opinion, Nevada's casino culture is responsible for this trend, and evidence from other casino-friendly states seems to support the contention that casinos attract problem gamblers. Some state governments are taking this destructive problem seriously and funding treatment programs, but Friess argues that more needs to be done. Friess is a Las Vegas-based freelance writer whose work appears regularly in national periodicals such as USA Today, Wired, *and* Newsweek.

As you read, consider the following questions:

1. Who is Dennis Nolan and what legislation was he trying to pass in 2005, as reported by Friess?

2. As the author notes, what percentage of Nevada's population is made up of problem gamblers, according to a
   2002 survey?
3. How many Gamblers Anonymous meetings take place
   each week in Las Vegas, according to the organization, as
   cited by Friess?

Frankie Suarez knows that had things worked out differ-
ently, she'd be comfortably retired now and finally taking
those European vacations her husband, Tony, had promised
her. Instead, she's still working in her late 60s, dishing out
food at a hospital cafeteria and relying on those meager wages
plus Social Security to pay her rent.

Tony Suarez shot himself to death in 1999, leaving behind
a wrenching note apologizing for the disaster he'd made of
their finances and their lives. His demise wasn't altogether a
surprise; Mrs. Suarez watched helplessly as he took two years
to squander their once considerable savings at the blackjack
table of a nearby casino since they moved here in the mid-
1990s from Baltimore.

"He had no control over it, I know that," she says quietly
from the modest 600-square-foot apartment they moved into
after the bank repossessed the 2,200-square-foot home they
built in 1996. "I just wish we [had] understood the problem
sooner. It all happened so fast. He had a problem and we did
not know what to do. Neither of us wanted to admit what was
happening."

The dark side of gambling—the urge to risk all again and
again—has led to untold numbers of cases like that of the
Suarez family. Such addiction is a nationwide problem, as
much a part of gambling as bright lights and ivory dice. But it
is particularly severe in Nevada, and it is starting to draw attention from local leaders.

Recognizing the Problem

[In 2005], in a move welcomed not just by gambling-addiction advocates but also by the casino industry itself, the [Nevada] governor proposed $100,000 a year in his two-year budget for treatment programs. Some state legislators plan to increase that figure to at least $1 million a year. And [in March 2005], the state officially acknowledged the annual National Problem Gambling Awareness Week for the first time.

"I think we've just acclimated ourselves and grown accustomed to the problem but now we're realizing how it negatively impacts not only the image of gambling but other lives as well," says State Sen. Dennis Nolan, a Las Vegas Republican whose [2005] bill would put $2 million into gambling-addiction treatment and prevention over two years. "While Nevada has been the innovator of the gambling industry, this is one area [where] we've fallen behind."

If the legislature puts up any money for treatment, it will be the first time the Silver State has specifically earmarked anything for this problem despite a 74-year history of legalized gambling. Seventeen other states have already done so, led by Indiana spending $3.5 million and Illinois, Connecticut, Iowa, Louisiana, and Oregon each spending roughly $2 million a year. New Jersey, which is most similar to Vegas with its Atlantic City boardwalk, spends $700,000 a year. Such efforts are aimed at a daunting challenge.

Following the Spread of Casinos

A Nevada-funded study revealed in 2002 that 6.4 percent of the state's population were either pathological or problem gamblers. That's far ahead of the 2.7 percent of the national population found to have such addictions in a 1998 survey conducted by National Gambling Impact Study Commission, a panel appointed by Congress. While no comprehensive state-by-state statistics are available, similar studies in other states

Casinos Target Gambling Addicts

Does the gaming industry target addicts? "It's like asking, Does the vodka industry target alcoholics?" says Henry Lesieur, head of the Institute for Problem Gambling. "Well, they target heavy drinkers, and a certain percentage are alcoholics."

Duke [University] professors Charles Clotfelter and Philip Cook did a study that found that 10% of lottery players account for 68% of lottery purchases. Similarly, [University of] Illinois professor [Earl] Grinols estimates that one-third to one-half of casino revenue comes from problem or pathological gamblers. "After a while [some casinos] don't want compulsive gamblers because they overrun their credit," Lesieur says. "But by then they've already made a lot of money off of them."

Perhaps more disturbing are cases where casinos allow known addicts to continue betting. After losing a million dollars, Houston businessman Joe McNeely sent a letter to several Louisiana casinos asking that they not allow him to gamble. But that didn't prevent him from losing another $2 million. McNeely then sued five casinos, claiming they continued to market to him aggressively even after they were aware of his addiction. Representatives of one casino, he says, even showed up at his mother's funeral and invited him to stop by. Though the casinos pointed out that McNeely hadn't registered with the state police, which has a self-banning system in place for addicts, they settled the suit for an undisclosed amount.

Brian O'Keefe, July 17, 2000. www.smartmoney.com.

have shown rates of 2.1 percent in North Dakota and 4.9 percent in Mississippi, according to the National Council on Problem Gambling.

"One not unexpected result was that the prevalence rate in Nevada was higher than in virtually every other state that we looked at," said Rachel Volberg, a gambling-impact researcher based in Northampton, Mass., who spearheaded the Nevada study. "That obviously speaks to the impact of exposure."

All this comes as legalized gambling continues to spread. Only Hawaii and Utah have no form of gambling, and voters in Broward County, Fla., approved a measure to allow slot machines at racetracks and a jai-alai fronton in an effort to save the sinking parimutuel [betting] industry.

Gambling addiction stories are as common in Nevada as tornado tales are in Kansas. Senator Nolan, in fact, became an advocate for such treatment after seeing his wife's sister left destitute by her gambling-addicted husband.

There are 100 meetings a week of Gamblers Anonymous in Las Vegas, far more than in other regions, according to Gamblers Anonymous.

"Just about everybody in Nevada knows or has a story just like I have," Nolan says. "Somebody knows somebody who has a problem gambling. It's part of our life here."

The $200,000 proposed in the two-year budget of Nevada Gov. Kenny Guinn comes as a result of Ms. Volberg's findings, said Guinn spokesman Greg Bortolin. He acknowledged it's not a large sum but insisted it's a start and that the governor believes the casino industry ought to be taking the lead on the matter.

Casinos Are Part of the Solution

Yet most of the money currently spent on gambling treatment in Nevada does come from what some see as an unlikely source: the casino conglomerates themselves. Several have taken up the issue to demonstrate good corporate citizenship and soften gambling's shady image, says Station Casinos spokeswoman Lesley Pittman, whose company owns 10 non-

Strip casinos that cater to local Las Vegans. Station Casinos donates about $250,000 a year to research and treatment programs, Ms. Pittman says.

Caesars Entertainment, which owns three resorts on the Las Vegas Strip, goes one step further, requiring all employees to report guests who have made comments that suggest they may be addicted to gambling or may be running into a serious financial or personal problem brought on by gambling. The casino maintains a list, now 2,500 names long, of customers who they suspect have gambling problems and who are no longer permitted to play in their casinos, said spokesman Robert Stewart.

"It's truly not good business to cater to problem gamblers because these are people whose addiction is progressive and will end in some destructive way," says Carol O'Hare, executive director of the Nevada Council on Problem Gambling, whose $445,000 annual budget is largely funded by donations from casinos. "The problem gambler is not a long-term customer. He's not profitable. Ultimately he becomes a casualty."

While many praise Guinn and Nolan's effort, they also complain it's a fraction of what's necessary. Ron Lawrence, founder of the nonprofit Community Counseling Center in Las Vegas, estimates that 5 percent of his 5,000 clients a year have gambling problems and that he could use the $100,000 himself to hire about three more counselors to handle the burden.

"This is a drop in the bucket," says Mr. Lawrence, who suggests a more realistic figure for a state with Nevada's gambling problems would be $3 million a year. "We need much more. This is Nevada, after all."

> *"Harrah's program ... requires workers
> such as dealers and cashiers to notify a
> manager if they believe a person has a
> gambling problem."*

Casinos Are Helping Curb Compulsive Gambling

Liz Benston

Liz Benston is a writer for the Las Vegas Sun *and its sister publication,* In Business Las Vegas. *In the following viewpoint, Benston describes how Harrah's casinos are implementing a new program to target and monitor problem gamblers. Instead of passively posting hotline numbers and providing pamphlets, Harrah's program seeks out problem gamblers on the casino floor and compels managers to sit down with these patrons to discuss treatment options. Benston notes that some experts are skeptical that the program will work as planned, but all agree that any type of intervention is beneficial in curbing the problem of pathological gambling.*

As you read, consider the following questions:

1. As Benston writes, what are all casinos required by law to do to deter problem gambling?

Liz Benston, "When Casinos Decide You're Losing Too Much Money," *Las Vegas Sun*, August 28, 2006. Reproduced by permission.

2. According to Harrah's ambassadors, as cited by the author, when is the right time to approach gamblers to initiate conversation about possible gambling problems?

3. According to Benston, what reservations does psychologist Henry Lesieur have about Harrah's ambassador program?

The Harrah's casino in Reno [Nevada] expects to see one of its regulars in the next few days.

But this man won't receive the typical welcome when he walks through the door.

Instead, a Harrah's casino manager will approach him and bring up an unpleasant topic: recent comments the man made to a casino host about refinancing his house and gambling with his retirement money.

After expressing concern, the manager will give the man a problem-gambling hotline number and a chance to enter himself into a database that will stop mailers from being sent to his home, among other self-help services.

The unidentified man is an unwitting participant in a program that casino giant Harrah's Entertainment implemented [in 2006] that is believed to be the first and most aggressive problem gambling effort of its kind in the country.

The "ambassador" program—taking its name from the casino managers charged with approaching gamblers with information about programs many casinos have offered for years—has captured the attention of problem gambling treatment experts normally skeptical of casino efforts to help compulsive gamblers.

Casinos in Nevada and many other states are required by law to post problem gambling hotline numbers, offer self-help pamphlets and educate casino workers about warning signs. Harrah's also allows gamblers to sign up on a "self-exclusion" list that applies to all of its casinos nationwide. These efforts,

How Self-Exclusion Lists Work

Self-exclusion lists differ between the states but share the same basic principles. Michigan, New Jersey, Indiana, Missouri, Illinois, and Mississippi have all adopted legislation and or regulations establishing voluntary self-exclusion lists for problem gamblers. . . .

All persons wishing to join the self-exclusion list must provide identification credentials.

Each state is different on the specifics, but generally requires a picture, physical description, social security number, address, and telephone number. The programs only allow the person wishing to enter the program to put themselves on the list. With the exclusion of an extreme circumstance, the programs also require the person to physically meet with gaming personnel in order to complete the procedure. Once a person has provided all necessary information and is listed on the state's program, the gaming commission or program administrator provides the information to the licensed casinos throughout the state. . . .

Once a person is caught in violation of the self-exclusion agreement, the person is removed from the gambling establishment. Depending on the laws in each state the person may then be prosecuted for criminal trespassing.

Winnings and losses by the self-excluded person are either confiscated or subject to forfeiture to the state gaming commission or board. Most states donate the confiscated money to charities that provide education and treatment to problem gamblers.

Andy Rhea, Gaming Law Review, *2005.*

which acknowledge problem gambling as a legitimate mental health disorder similar to alcoholism, require gamblers to take the first step themselves.

The Harrah's program is different, experts say, because it requires workers such as dealers and cashiers to notify a manager if they believe a person has a gambling problem. The manager then calls the "ambassador" on duty to handle the touchy task of sitting down with the customer.

Competitors say the responsibility to help gamblers already lies with every rank-and-file employee on the casino floor as part of state-mandated training programs.

In reality, problem gambling advocates say, workers are being told about the disease but are rarely taking the initiative to intercept people on the casino floor.

"Frankly, there's a lot of lip service at the corporate level that doesn't get translated down to the employees," said Keith Whyte, executive director of the National Council on Problem Gambling. "I can't tell you the number of times I've gone into a casino and have found brochures tucked away and employees who don't know what their responsibilities are. There's a difference between having a program and making sure employees are comfortable enough to take action."

Previously, workers didn't feel at ease approaching people who probably needed help, said Andy Donato, a casino supervisor at Harrah's Reno and one of about 700 "ambassadors" who have volunteered for the added responsibility nationwide.

"This program reassures them that we really believe in this," Donato said.

The program requires employees to take action based on what a person says. Casinos and some treatment experts believe that unless a gambler's behavior is over the top, words are a more definitive indicator of a person's mental state.

There aren't any specific "trigger" phrases—that's left to employees' judgment. Workers receive several hours of training that includes watching instructional videos with interactions between employees and distraught customers.

"We don't want to shoehorn them into a box so that they're thinking, 'If I don't hear this phrase then I don't need to help the person,'" said Harrah's spokesman David Strow.

So far, about two to three such conversations have occurred at each Harrah's property per month. Gamblers don't appear to be resisting efforts to strike up a conversation, though in some cases, ambassadors find that the best time to approach them is not right away but after the person has had time to cool off from his last gambling session.

Some appreciate the information and concern but do not appear to need help, while others have been referred to treatment as a result of the program, Strow said.

Donato said he received input from outside problem gambling and human resources experts on how to approach people in a friendly way without making them feel defensive or combative.

For example, a Harrah's manager might approach a gambler and suggest a "timeout" over a drink or a meal.

"I've been with Harrah's almost 30 years, and over the years you hear all sorts of statements, like, 'My wife is going to kill me when I go home' to 'I'm having a bad day, I never should have come here,'" Donato said. "It's not easy to evaluate without talking to the person directly whether the person is serious."

Henry Lesieur, a staff psychologist at Rhode Island Hospital's gambling treatment program and one of the nation's foremost treatment experts, calls the effort "one of the most thought-out programs I've seen" from a casino company.

Lesieur, who co-authored the first definition of problem gambling included in the American Psychiatric Association's diagnostic manual, said discussing self-help schemes with gamblers in the casino is an "improvement." However, he questions Harrah's commitment to maintaining a growing "watch" list documenting conversations and outcomes involving hundreds, even thousands of gamblers for years to come.

131

The program also is not going to catch each gambler who tries to re-enter casinos after requesting that they be excluded or refused service from Harrah's properties, he added.

Some problem gambling experts are skeptical that the program will make a difference for gamblers in the throes of addiction.

Robert Hunter, clinical director of the Problem Gambling Center in Las Vegas, said Harrah's may have trouble reasoning with addicts in a gambling environment.

"If someone at a bar has had too many drinks, that's not the time to talk to someone about their drinking," Hunter said. "I see folks who've already crossed the line into addiction. For them, this is not going to be much help. That said, I support any efforts to get people into recovery."

Carol O'Hare, director of the Nevada Council on Problem Gambling, says the program still represents a "big step" for the industry because it aims to help people before they hit bottom.

Lesieur says the program is a sign that the industry is willing to face its Achilles heel head-on rather than be pummeled by critics.

Strow said the effort resulted from a policy of continuous evaluation and improvement based on new research. It is not a knee-jerk reaction or an admission of inadequacy of past programs, he said.

Lesieur, though, said the program does not go far enough.

The responsibility to be more proactive lies with state governments, not Harrah's, he said.

"Harrah's is in the business of making money," he said. "I don't expect them to have a hard sell. If any education of gambling is to be done, it needs to be done by the state."

Periodical Bibliography

The following articles have been selected to supplement the diverse views presented in this chapter.

Associated Press   "Popular Parkinson's Drug Linked to Gambling: Compulsive Behaviors May Be Side Effect of Mirapex, Research Suggests," July 12, 2005. www.msnbc.msn.com.

Victoria Clayton   "High Stakes for Teen Gamblers," *MSNBC*, February 6, 2006. www.msnbc.msn.com.

Stephen Elliott   "Swimming with the Online Card Sharks," *Salon*, May 2, 2002. www.salon.com.

Jeff Evans   "For Women, Gambling Turns Pathological Faster," *Clinical Psychiatry News*, August 2004.

Marsha King   "Older Adults Vulnerable to Gambling Addiction," *Seattle Times*, November 28, 2005.

Jeffrey Kluger   "When Gambling Becomes Obsessive: For Millions, the Thrill of the Bet Is as Addictive as Any Drug," *Time*, August 1, 2005.

G. Jeffrey MacDonald   "Will Teens Know When to Fold in the Popular Poker Craze?" *Christian Science Monitor*, December 22, 2004.

National Center for Responsible Gaming   "Harvard Survey Shows Rate of College Gambling Lower than Previous Estimates," August 14, 2004. www.ncrg.org.

Mattathias Schwartz   "The Hold-'em Holdup," *New York Times Magazine*, June 11, 2006.

Marianne Szegedy-Maszak   "The Worst of All Bets," *U.S. News & World Report*, May 23, 2005.

Nathan Thornburgh   "Parents for Poker," *Time*, October 2, 2006.

Richard E. Vatz and Lee S. Weinberg   "Gambling, Psychology, and State Politics," *USA Today* (magazine), May 2003.

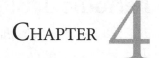

CHAPTER 4

How Are Lottery Innovations Affecting Society and the Gaming Industry?

Chapter Preface

In America's ever-changing economic landscape, all industries that want to survive adapt to meet the fluctuating demands of consumers. The gambling industry is no exception. Commercial casinos attempt to lure patrons with increasingly appealing computer-based gaming machines that feature beloved celebrities and trendy themes. State lotteries have been contemplating the sale of online lottery tickets in order to reach a broader market that has quick, wireless Internet connections. The racing industry, however, is the segment of the gaming industry that stands to benefit the most from innovations in the way it conducts business.

While some racetracks—such as the famed Churchill Downs, home of the Kentucky Derby—have continued to perform consistently throughout the years, a number of smaller, less historic tracks have increasingly fallen on hard times. In an attempt to aid the failing tracks, industry managers turned to the concept of the racino in the 1990s. Racinos are racetracks that operate casino-style gambling on the premises in hopes of bringing in more customers than racing alone can attract. West Virginia opened the nation's first racino in 1990 when the owners of Mountaineer Race Track installed banks of slot machine–style devices. The devices were not the iconic "one-armed bandit" slot machines typical of commercial casinos; instead the chosen slotlike device was termed a video lottery terminal, or VLT, an electronic gaming machine tied to the state's lottery. The state lottery board runs the VLTs, and proceeds are divided between the state and the host track. Other states experimenting with racinos have also embraced VLTs, while a few have opted for traditional slot machines owned and operated by the tracks themselves.

With much of the revenue collected from the VLTs going directly to state governments, the positive effects of the new racino hybrids have been hotly contested. Proponents argue that simply getting more patrons to the racetrack is a positive influence, and in turn will increase overall revenue for the racing industry. For example, a study released by students at the University of Arizona in 2003 determined that racinos attracted better breeds of horses and paid out higher purses. Many skeptics, however, still question the actual benefits of the racinos, noting that in the 2003 study, the results were not so overwhelmingly positive as to support the introduction of casino gaming at all tracks throughout the country.

While much of the debate concerning racinos centers on the economic impact on the racing industry, communities raise other concerns, such as the potential increase in crime, bankruptcy, and suicide rates, whenever tracks propose to convert to racinos. Nevertheless, as of 2006, eleven states have found the potential benefits of racinos to be irresistible. This revolution in the racing industry exemplifies one way in which the gambling industry has continued to evolve in order to retain its customers. The authors in the following chapter debate the impact of different innovations in the gambling industry and their economic and social effects.

> "The VLTs are the fastest of all forms of gambling to result in addiction-like behaviours."

Video Lottery Terminals Are Addictive and Destructive

Sol Boxenbaum

Sol Boxenbaum is the CEO and president of Viva Consulting Family Life, Inc., a nonprofit organization in Canada dedicated to raising awareness about the problems associated with pathological gambling. In the following viewpoint Boxenbaum claims that video lottery terminals (VLTs) pose a greater risk of addiction than do well-known culprits such as tobacco, alcohol, and heroin. He cites examples and statistics specific to the Canadian province of Quebec, which is home to more than fourteen thousand government-operated VLTs and has experienced a significant number of gambling-related suicides.

As you read, consider the following questions:

1. What false impression do VLTs give players, according to Boxenbaum?

2. In the author's opinion, how do pathological gamblers convince themselves that gambling on VLTs is not about the money won or lost?

Sol Boxenbaum, "Quebec Report," Viva Consulting Family Life, Inc., 2003. Reproduced by permission.

3. In what way are experiments on conditioning the behavior of rats comparable to gamblers playing VLTs, in Boxenbaum's view?

Prior to this era of high technology, who would have thought there could be something more addictive than tobacco, alcohol, or even heroin? This addiction is not ingested, leaves no odors or visible signs, yet, despite all efforts by its victims to abstain, leaves them powerless. It is called a Video Lottery Terminal (VLT). Even more surprising is the fact that this devastating piece of equipment is owned, operated, and regulated by our [Canadian] government. The basic difference between a VLT and a slot machine, which can be found only in casinos, is the easy access one has to discover the VLT, and the ability to slip in and out of the 3,828 licensed establishments, around the province [of Quebec], where these machines can be played. One can play them on [one's] lunch hour, coffee break, on the way to or from work without having to make a trip to the casino. The VLT has broken the gender barrier as well, in that women previously would not go into a bar unescorted, but it is viewed as being normal for a woman to play the VLTs. If the government had its way, with no criticism from consumer protectors like myself and others, the machines would also be in convenience stores, service stations, etc., in the community. After all, the Nintendo, Genesis, Playstation generation are natural targets for this type of activity. There will always be unscrupulous bar owners who look the other way while minors try to beat the electronic monster. When the smoke clears at the end of each day, the government pulls 1.895 million dollars out of the marketplace and into general revenue. We are expected to believe that our communities benefit from this, of course, because our government provides the greatest healthcare system and the highest quality educational institutions in the country. Every month, welfare and old-age pension cheques get recycled in the 14,713 VLTs around our province. One needs only to look at all the

C'MON IN RUDOLPH, THESE AIN'T NO REINDEER GAMES.

© CartoonStock.com

empty stores that used to be viable businesses. The quickest growing industries today seem to be pawn shops and cheque-cashing agencies.

Addiction and Intermittent Reward

While excessive gambling is a stupid activity, the people who become pathological gamblers are not stupid. Addictions are equal opportunity employers, and the VLTs are the fastest of all forms of gambling to result in addiction-like behaviours. Gamblers don't realize that these machines were created by electronic engineers, systems analysts, computer whizzes, mathematicians, statisticians, product design engineers, and psychologists. The machines give the false impression that the player has an influence on the outcome of play by allowing them to stop the spin quickly or let it go through the natural cycle, but the reality is that they are playing against a random-number-generating computer chip. The result of each spin is predetermined every time the spin button is depressed. The odds of winning on any spin is identical to the odds of winning on subsequent spins, and the amount of money inserted or time spent has no bearing on the result. The chances of winning on any machine are identical, and the odds (prize payout) are grossly disproportionate to the probability of winning. The maximum payout is five hundred dollars, yet people will lose thousands of dollars trying to win that "jackpot". The reason for that is because, as most pathological gamblers will admit, it's no longer about money. The VLTs offer an escape from reality and from the physical and mental pains of everyday living. These machines create equality in that there is no skill required, no communicating with others, instant gratification, and intermittent rewards. And most frightening of all is the fact that pathological gamblers do not have the ability to stop. The VLT is so addictive that these gamblers have to keep on hitting that button, like a laboratory rat which has been conditioned to expect intermittent rewards. The partial reinforcement effect, which has been repeatedly demonstrated in laboratories, contributes to the disorder. More specifically, an experimenter places a rat on a food deprivation routine until there is a 10–20% reduction in weight. The rat is then placed in a box and is trained to press the lever for food: every time it presses the lever a pellet of food drops into a tray. Once the association between pressing the lever and receiving the food is made, the experimenter changes the program so that not every response is reinforced. Reinforcement can come after 15 presses, or maybe 3 presses, or 25 presses. The rat may press for 20 seconds, or 5 seconds, or 60 seconds. Reinforcement is not delivered predictably. Under this condition, rats produce a steady high rate of lever pressing. Behaviour learned under partial reinforcement takes a longer time to extinguish. The fact that the VLT also dispenses reinforcement on an intermittent or unpredictable basis means that the player is subject to the same principle as the rat. The player wins some of the time and doesn't always lose: this perpetuates gambling behaviour. These gamblers only seek help after they have hit rock bottom and have no more alternatives. Sadly, some take their own life, seeing only helplessness and hopelessness.

The High Toll of Compulsive Gambling

Pathological gambling has the highest attempted suicide rate of all addictions. Since the coroner started compiling data, there have been 109 gambling related suicides in Quebec, at least 49 [between 1998 and 2000]. These deaths are definitive only because a suicide note was left, or because the victim's family reported that gambling was the problem. How many other victims did not leave a note, and because pathological gambling is such a hidden addiction, the family was not aware of the problem? How many suicides appear to be accidental deaths? Some despondent gamblers do not want to burden their families with the knowledge that they have taken their own life, and yet others want their family to be able to collect benefits from life insurance policies.

If we are to attempt to control the madness of VLT addiction, we must not allow the government to continue practicing mind control over even more unfortunate victims. We must see a dramatic reduction in the number of machines, a stop to the easy access to machines, and sincere efforts to educate the people, with an extra emphasis on those most vulnerable: our youth, our minorities, and our senior citizens. And we must see treatment made available for those who already have become pathological gamblers and victims of Loto-Quebec's [the lottery company's] greed.

| "Gambling revenues . . . have become a
critical stream of income in a number
of states."

Video Lottery Terminals Provide Economic Benefits for States

Fox Butterfield

In the following viewpoint, Fox Butterfield states that gambling revenues compose a significant portion of states' incomes and that a large share of these gambling revenues is collected from state-run video lottery terminals (VLTs). He notes that while the original intent of using the machines was to help bolster flagging racetrack revenues in many states, the popularity and growth of the industry has allowed states to become dependent on this income. Butterfield, a journalist at the New York Times, *has written books on a wide range of topics.*

As you read, consider the following questions:

1. What benefits does Butterfield say Rhode Island and South Dakota have been able to pass on to taxpayers as a result of increased gambling revenue?

2. According to the author, what danger are the states that rely on gambling revenue now facing?

3. According to Butterfield, what traditional form of revenue have gambling profits surpassed in Rhode Island, and what services do these monies help fund?

Gambling revenues, once a mere trickle, have become a critical stream of income in a number of states, in some cases surpassing traditional sources like the corporate income tax and helping states lower personal income or property taxes.

The sums are so alluring that some officials are concerned that their states are becoming as addicted as problem gamblers. "We're drunk on gambling revenue," said Representative Wayne A. Smith, the Republican who is House majority leader in the Delaware Legislature. "Gambling revenues are like free money."

A Vital Source of Revenue

In Rhode Island, South Dakota, Louisiana, Oregon and, most of all, Nevada, taxes from casinos, slot machines at racetracks and lotteries make up more than 10 percent of overall revenues, according to a [2005] report. In Delaware, West Virginia, Indiana, Iowa and Mississippi, gambling revenues are fast approaching 10 percent.

So vital has the money become that in Rhode Island, gambling revenue has surpassed the corporate income tax to become the state's third largest source of income, after the personal income and sales tax. It has enabled the state to avoid raising its income tax for 10 years.

Because of gambling, South Dakota officials were able to push through a 20 percent reduction in property taxes a decade ago by increasing to 50 percent the state's share of gambling revenue from video lottery terminals, up from 37 percent.

A property tax reduction was also the main argument in Pennsylvania for legalizing gambling when the Legislature [in 2004] authorized slot machines at racetracks and casinos after years of intense opposition.

A Fair Percentage of State Revenue

In Delaware, where video slot machines were legalized in 1994 as a way to revive ailing horse racing and horse farming industries, racetracks are thriving, horse farms have been preserved and the legislature, unexpectedly, has been able to cut the top personal income tax rate over several years during the late 1990's to 5.9 percent, from 8.4 percent, a reduction of nearly one-third.

The scenes that fuel Delaware's success take place every night. On a recent cold, rainy weeknight, many of the 2,500 video slot machines at Dover Downs were clinking steadily, as customers from as far as Baltimore, Washington and Richmond, Va., pressed the play button every three seconds, as fast as the electronic terminals can spin. That was good news for the state, since Dover Downs, a combination harness racetrack, Las Vegas-style hotel, slot machine emporium and Nascar track, pumped $102 million from its slot machines alone into the budget [in 2004]. Delaware over all got $222 million from gambling—8.1 percent of its $2.72 billion in state revenues.

Gambling in Neighboring States Threatens Revenue

But Delaware, like most states that rely on gambling revenue, now faces a danger—competition from nearby states for the same dollars.

Some 70 percent of gambling losses in Delaware's three "racinos," racetracks with video slot machines, come from visitors from Pennsylvania and Maryland, according to the Delaware Department of Finance. But Pennsylvania legalized

Why Most States Adopted Lotteries

Lotteries spread rapidly in this country during the 1970s and 1980s, when New Hampshire [the first state to enact a modern lottery in 1964] seemed a model to many states. In 1978 California voters passed Proposition 13, which placed severe restrictions on the state's taxing authority and inspired voters in some other states to enact similar measures. More important, Prop 13 and its progeny made politicians everywhere averse to new taxes. Only one state, Connecticut, has enacted a personal income tax or general sales tax since 1977. Ronald Reagan was elected president in 1980 on a promise to make substantial reductions in federal income tax rates. He not only accomplished this goal but also persuaded Congress to reduce spending on grant programs to the states.

To state governments caught in a vise between greater revenue needs and widespread opposition to taxes, the lottery seemed an appealing way out. . . . In all, [forty-two] state governments and the District of Columbia . . . now own and operate lotteries.

Michael Nelson, American Prospect, *June 4, 2001.*

slot machines [in 2004] and the Maryland Legislature is debating a bill to legalize gambling there.

If Pennsylvania and Maryland install all the slot machines they are considering, Delaware could lose $120 million annually, almost 5 percent of state revenues, said Tom Cook, a spokesman for the Department of Finance.

In Dover, the looming battle with Pennsylvania and Maryland has touched off a debate pitting the governor, Ruth Ann Minner, against many legislators.

"We have legislators every day who propose opening new venues, like a big casino on the waterfront in Wilmington or a floating barge in the Delaware River," said Governor Minner, a Democrat. "But there are only so many dollars that are going to be spent on gambling, and I don't want to build that into the base of my budget and then find Pennsylvania and Maryland leaving a $120 million hole in it."

So Governor Minner has decided, in her words, "to draw a line in the sand." She has allowed longer hours at the state's three racinos and encouraged them to modernize to attract out-of-state bettors. But she is saying no to stand-alone casinos or other proposed new forms of gambling like blackjack tables and sports betting.

South Dakota Dependent on Gambling Income

Similar dilemmas are cropping up around the country now that 48 states, with the exception of Utah and Hawaii, have legalized some form of gambling.

Like Delaware, South Dakota first legalized gambling for a limited purpose—allowing casinos in the decaying frontier town of Deadwood to try to preserve it.

But South Dakota now gets $112.8 million a year from gambling, most of it from video slot machines in bars all over the state operated by the state lottery. Gambling accounts for 13.2 percent of South Dakota's revenue, according to state figures.

David Knudson, a Republican state senator from Sioux Falls, concedes that gambling has brought some benefits. In 1995 he was chief of staff to then Gov. Bill Janklow when South Dakota was able to push through the 20 percent property tax reduction because of gambling revenue.

"But that only increased our dependence on gambling," Mr. Knudson said. He noted that gambling opponents often cite the danger of addiction for individual gamblers, and said, "But the biggest addict turns out to be the state government that becomes dependent on it."

In 2000, worried about an increase in divorces, crime and suicide among problem gamblers, Mr. Knudson supported a ballot issue to repeal the law legalizing the state lottery video slot machines. But many members of the Legislature argued that the state would have to come up with alternative sources of money, Senator Knudson said, and the measure was defeated.

Iowa, Pioneer of Riverboat Gambling

Iowa, which pioneered modern riverboat gambling in 1989 when it legalized gambling as long as the boats were cruising on a river, is continually striving to keep ahead of neighboring states. When Illinois and Missouri soon passed similar laws, the Iowa Legislature voted to add slot machines at racetracks. It also negotiated with local Indian tribes for tribal casinos.

[In 2004], facing a $140 million budget gap that threatened education programs, Iowa added table gambling at racetracks, dropped a moratorium on new gambling licenses and allowed gambling on the riverboats when they were tied ashore.

Iowa derives 6.65 percent of its state revenue from gambling, according to a new study by William N. Thompson, a professor of public administration at the University of Nevada, Las Vegas, and a colleague at the university, Christopher Stream.

The analysis, which Mr. Thompson says is the first to measure the percentage of state revenue from gambling, was done for the Wisconsin Policy Research Institute, a business-sponsored organization, and based on 2003 data.

Nevada, not surprisingly, gets by far the largest proportion of its revenue from gambling, 42.6 percent, Professor Thompson found. South Dakota is second, with 13.2 percent.

Gambling Revenue Serves Multiple Purposes

Rhode Island is another state that legalized video slot machines for a limited purpose—to help its aging horse and dog racing tracks. When the slots were introduced in 1992, the income was small, but the amount has almost doubled every year since, said Joseph A. Montalbano, the president of the Rhode Island Senate, and has reached $281 million a year, including the state's conventional lottery.

Not only has gambling revenue surpassed the corporate income tax in Rhode Island and enabled the state to avoid raising its income tax, gambling also helps teach children, pay for medical care for the poor and repair roads.

But Rhode Island, too, faces competition. There is concern that Massachusetts, the source of many customers at Rhode Island's racinos, will legalize slot machines at its own racetracks, and within an hour's drive of Providence, the large Indian-owned casinos in Connecticut are expanding.

"We're in a Catch-22 situation, with our third-largest revenue source being surrounded by these other gambling facilities," said Senator Montalbano, a Democrat. . . .

In Dover, Denis McGlynn, president and chief executive of Dover Downs Gaming and Entertainment Inc., also sees the need to expand, perhaps by allowing his slots to stay open 24 hours a day instead of closing at 4 A.M.

"Sometimes you play the cards you're dealt," said Mr. McGlynn, whose company has prospered with the legalization of gambling in Delaware and is now a publicly owned corporation. "Delaware is small. It's not Silicon Valley. People are not pouring in to build new industries from the ground up. But people are willing to come here and gamble and contribute to the state's revenues."

"While the fan base for thoroughbreds is dwindling, tracks where casino-style gambling is allowed are doing well."

Racinos Benefit the Horse-Racing Industry

Greg Melikov

In the following viewpoint, Greg Melikov, a writer and editor who lives in Texas, argues that his state's racetracks need more lucrative ways to stay competitive against other popular gaming entertainments. As Melikov notes, other states have saved their racing industries by combining racetracks with casino-style slot machines and video lottery terminal (VLT) parlors. The resulting hybrid "racinos" rake in millions off the state-run VLTs, and the profits are shared by the government, the track, and the racing prize winners. Melikov argues that Texas horse racing could likewise benefit from the inclusion of slots and VLTs at the state's tracks.

As you read, consider the following questions:

1. As Melikov reports, what was the first innovation to rescue horse racing's declining revenues in the late 1980s and 1990s?

Greg Melikov, "Success of Horse Racing Depends on Slots: Tracks in States Like Texas and Florida Struggling," Associated Content, June 26, 2005. www.associatedcontent .com. Reproduced by permission.

2. According to the author, what effect are racinos in Oklahoma and New Mexico having on the Texas horse-racing industry?

3. What kinds of incentives has Retama Park used to lure patrons to the track since 1997, according to Melikov?

The future of horse racing depends on Las Vegas–type slot machines. While the fan base for thoroughbreds is dwindling, tracks where casino-style gambling is allowed are doing well.

The Sport of Kings [horse racing] after World War II lost out when fans embraced other sports such as pro baseball, football and basketball. Then lotteries blossomed around the country, siphoning dollars from tracks.

Enter casino gambling, thanks to flourishing Las Vegas, which has surpassed most vacation spots around the country.

What hurt racing until simulcasting [broadcasting races in real time] emerged [in the late 1980s] was that if you couldn't visit the track of your choice, you couldn't wager unless you went the bookie route. Now there's online wagering and betting by phone. Simulcasting rescued tracks fighting to survive.

Slots Inflate Prize Winnings and State Revenues

Slot machines are picking up where simulcasting left off. A case in point, Louisiana tracks that have them are doing much better than Texas tracks that don't. That's because purses for racing climb as revenue from video slots rolls in.

Texas lawmakers [in 2005] refused to act on a bill to allow a statewide vote that would allow slots at horse and dog tracks around the state. Proponents vow to continue the fight because they say the future of Texas racing is at stake.

But the road to slots in some states is not without potholes. For example, Gulfstream Park in South Florida looked like it would benefit when voters in Broward County approved a referendum.

But the Florida Legislature adjourned in May [2005] after the House and Senate passed dramatically different bills. Those differences weren't reconciled and, to make matters worse, there [we]re no plans for a special session [later that] year.

This prompted Gulfstream, two dog tracks and a jai-alai fronton to sue the state in Broward to clarify if they are authorized to operate slot machines. Meanwhile, gambling opponents several days earlier in Tallahassee asked a trial judge to rule that the pari-mutuels [betting pools] cannot start offering slot machines without an enabling law from the Legislature.

The Broward referendum that passed in March [2005] required the Legislature to OK a bill by July 1. Gov. Jeb Bush and Florida's Native-American tribes, many of which operate casinos in the state, opposed the referendum. [Racinos eventually opened in Florida in 2006.]

Slots Are a Draw to Gamblers

Quite a few tracks have been resurrected because the machines attract gamblers and common folks.

A case in point: Louisiana tracks that have them are doing much better than Texas tracks that don't. In fact, other neighboring states such as Oklahoma and New Mexico are attracting Texas horse owners, trainers and jockeys as well as Lone Star State residents looking for action.

Since slots were introduced at New Mexico tracks in 1999, horse breeding operations have soared to record numbers, fueling big increases in employment and salaries in all areas of its racing industry. The opposite is true of Texas.

For instance, Retama Park, a horse track in Greater San Antonio, is having a difficult time since the 9/11 tragedy. From '95 to '00, on-track mutuel handle for quarter horses and thoroughbreds climbed steadily. Simulcasting wagering also rose.

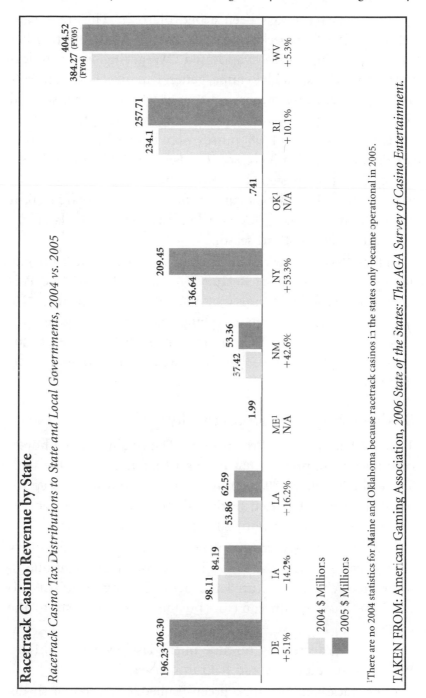

Racetrack Casino Revenue by State

Racetrack Casino Tax Distributions to State and Local Governments, 2004 vs. 2005

404.52 (FY05)
384.27 (FY04)
WV +5.3%

257.71
234.1
RI +10.1%

.741
OK[1] N/A

209.45
136.64
NY +53.3%

53.36
37.42
NM +42.6%

1.99
ME[1] N/A

62.59
53.86
LA +16.2%

98.11 84.19
IA −14.2%

196.23 206.30
DE +5.1%

2004 $ Millions
2005 $ Millions

[1]There are no 2004 statistics for Maine and Oklahoma because racetrack casinos in the states only became operational in 2005.

TAKEN FROM: American Gaming Association, *2006 State of the States: The AGA Survey of Casino Entertainment.*

But it hasn't always been a bed of roses. The track cancelled the last two weeks of its '95 quarter-horse meeting because operating funds evaporated. "Wagering was way less than projections," said Retama general manager Robert Pollock, a former horse owner and trainer who became a steward that year. Despite Retama Park filing for Chapter 9 bankruptcy on March 20, 1996, purses were boosted for the second season and wagering increased. On Feb. 13, 1997, a U.S. Bankruptcy Court judge signed an order confirming the city's reorganization and funding plan for the track. On March 26, it emerged from bankruptcy and less than six weeks later the track launched the third season.

Enter Bryan Brown, named chief executive officer on July 10, 1997. "The best asset Retama Park has is Bryan," said Pollock, who earlier that year was named general manager. "He has business sense and an easygoing manner. He's a great guy. Our strong suit is a really good management team. We put together the right people—that's why we're doing so good businesswise."

Business Improves Dramatically

Then all became rosy. Brown said, "The quality of the horses continues to improve—that means better racing for the fans. To be able to offer $100,000 in purses is also a major step for us. When we first started talking about it a few years ago, we thought it would take until 2002 to reach those numbers."

"We have increased our wagering and attendance every year since 1997," Brown said. "The bottom line: Continue to improve. We've restructured the debt. Cutting costs isn't always the answer. You can't do business cutting costs to the bone."

However, decreasing revenue in the last several years hurt, Pollock said. "Slot[s] would help immensely."

The track is named for a green-limbed, small tree or shrub, native to Texas, which can grow to 35 feet. Branches contain needle-sharp thorns—adorned by fragrant flowers with bright yellow petals. It has the reputation of being attractive and aggressive—plus hard to get rid of.

It appears Retama Park is aptly named. Promotional events such as 50-Cent Nights, the brainstorm of publicity/marketing director Doug Vair, were launched in '97 to keep patrons coming back during both meetings.

Fifty-Cent Fridays and Saturdays include free admission. Hotdogs, soda and programs are 50 cents. There's also $1 draft beer and free activities for kids featuring pony rides, a petting zoo, face painting and clowns.

Texas racing, however, is at a crossroads. Promotions won't bring horsemen back to race for lesser purses than neighboring states. But slots would.

> "This solution—of turning every race track into a casino—seems fatally flawed."

Racinos Hurt the Horse-Racing Industry

Joe Bob Briggs

Joe Bob Briggs is an author and columnist who writes about movies, Las Vegas, and other aspects of pop culture. In the following viewpoint, Briggs contends that the transformation of racetracks into racinos (racetracks with slot machine—usually video lottery terminals—parlors) may be bringing financial rewards but is damaging the integrity of racing. Briggs argues that slots gamblers and horse race bettors are two distinct types of gambler. Merging these two forms of gambling will not create more fans of racing, Briggs claims, but will simply turn tracks into casinos that happen to have racetracks attached.

As you read, consider the following questions:

1. Why were horse bettors at Louisiana Downs furious to find slot machines in the grandstand, according to Briggs?

2. In the author's view, how are slot machine players and horse bettors fundamentally different in their gambling?

3. How does Briggs suggest horse racing should be "strengthened" if racinos are to remain part of the sport?

When Louisiana Downs, the popular Shreveport race track, was given permission to install slot machines in 1993, they celebrated by scattering slots through three floors of the grandstand.

You were never more than five seconds away from a slot. You could walk from the betting window to the slot handle and back without missing a race or losing your machine. You could even watch the race on a video screen and continue playing the slots while the ponies ran.

And the whole scheme was a disaster.

The horse bettors were furious to have the slot noise in their sanctuary, and the slot players were angry about being treated like second-class citizens.

Ray Tromba, the manager of Louisiana Downs, had just learned the hard way what every other "racino" now recognizes: There's no way to integrate slot machines into a race track. Slots players and horse bettors are two entirely different species. Horseplayers don't play slots, and slots players don't bet horses.

At Louisiana Downs, they eventually moved all the slot machines to the first floor. The second, third and fourth were returned to the horse people. And now that the twain could never meet, except perhaps occasionally on the elevator, the business took off.

Slots Could Destroy Racing

At the [December 2002] Racing and Gaming Summit, where race track owners gathered to discuss how to maximize profit from slot machines, I got this gnawing feeling that they've given birth to some kind of Frankenstein's Monster that has nothing to do with racing and eventually could destroy it entirely. They're clutching at slot machines because live horse racing (and dog racing, for that matter) has been declining for the past 20 years. But this solution—of turning every race track into a casino—seems fatally flawed to me. By chasing after short-term profit, they might be driving nails into their own coffins.

Let's start with the basic nature of these two forms of gambling. Horse bettors start planning their gambling day 24 hours ahead of time. They buy the *Daily Racing Form* in the afternoon and study *tomorrow's* races. Reading a past performance chart in the *Racing Form* is not a simple task. There are hundreds of bits of information on each horse, all embedded in agate type, and the bits of information don't mean anything in isolation—they have to be compared to the other horses in the same race.

Most tracks average ten races a day. Then, if the bettor is also betting on other tracks via satellite feed, he could have as many as 70 races to study. Assuming about eight horses per race, that's 560 past performance charts to look at before he even makes his first betting decision. Then he has to decide which races to bet, how much to bet on each horse, which horses to bet in parlays [accumulated bets], and how high the odds need to be to make each bet worthwhile.

In other words, it's like cramming for a math final every night. And even then his job is not over. The serious bettor goes to the paddock before each race and looks his horses over to make sure they're not exhibiting any physical defects. Then he watches the tote board to make sure his horse doesn't get bet down to such low odds that the bet becomes worthless. The whole puzzle-solving process is labor-intensive and time-intensive.

Now let's examine the slot-machine player. His betting decision occurs two seconds before he decides to pull a particular handle on a particular machine. And if he decides he doesn't like the way the lights are flashing or the reels [are] lining up on that one, he simply moves to another machine. It's not labor-intensive, it's not time-intensive. It is, in fact, mindless pure chance.

Can there *be* two more different personality types? Whose idea was it to harness these groups together in the first place?

Hoping to Integrate Two Types of Gamblers

According to Mike Shagan, a business consultant and attorney who helped launch Off-Track Betting in the seventies, it was the state legislatures. "A race track is a benevolent facility to a politician," he said. "When you give a track the right to have slots, you are not creating a geographic expansion of gambling. It's a way to limit gambling but still provide benefits to racing. From the government point of view, the health of live racing is still important."

So the tracks accepted the slot machines as a way to compete for the gamblers who had been lost to casinos. But my question about this is: how can you lose a horse bettor to a casino in the first place, if, as we now know, a horseplayer is not really interested in games of pure chance? Over the two days of this conference, I was never able to find anyone who could adequately answer that. Could it be that the horse-racing product itself is what has driven gamblers away? And could it be that they didn't leave to chase gambling opportunites somewhere else, but just . . . left?

Still, hope springs eternal, and there are racing consultants out there who claim it's possible to take a slots player and make him into a horse bettor. "Long-term, I think you can integrate the two," says Saverio "Sal" Scheri III, Managing Director of WhiteSand Consulting. "We do have an opportunity to take folks and cross them over. And to do that, direct mail is king."

The Spread of Racinos in the United States and Canada

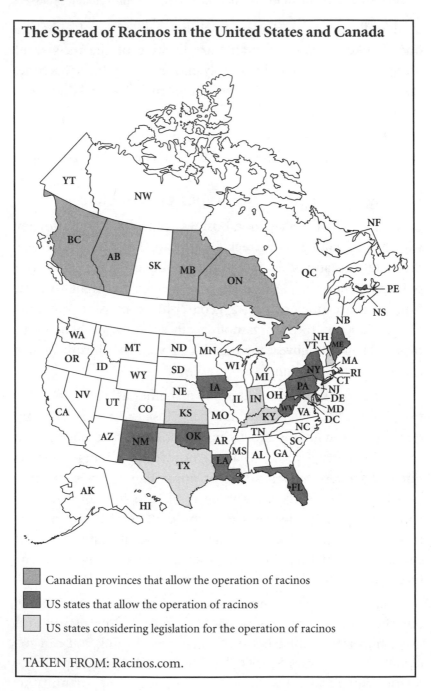

Canadian provinces that allow the operation of racinos

US states that allow the operation of racinos

US states considering legislation for the operation of racinos

TAKEN FROM: Racinos.com.

The idea here would be that the slots bettor constantly gets coupons in the mail that make it advantageous for him to place horse bets while he's at the track. Similarly, the horse bettor is comped with coupons tied to slots betting. The hope is that each will discover the charm of the other kind of betting.

I don't really buy this either, though, because I think all the gamblers already *know* about other forms of betting. Of the two possibilities, the more likely one is to convert a slots guy into a racing guy, simply because most simple bettors regard horse racing as arcane and hard to figure out. Anything that tends to make it painless is going to help—but a slots bettor is still likely to just choose the prettiest horse or some other decision like that, and that's a sure way to end up losing enough money to get burned out on the idea.

Bruce Wentworth, General Manager of the Dubuque (Iowa) Racing Association, says that he introduced 600 slots into his track as early as 1985, and to get "crossover" business, he scattered TV sets with racing feeds all over the slots floor. The sets have video but no audio. Still, he's had only limited success. "The customer wants to know 'How hard do you have to work to make this bet?'" he says. "The more complicated the game, the older the crowd."

No Proof That the System Works

David Pye, Vice President of Corporate Development for Scientific Games Corp., had a similar experience at the tracks in West Virginia, which was one of the first states to launch racinos.

"Our idea was to bring racing to the customer directly through the VLT [the slot machine screen itself]," he says. "The results of offering racing in the VLTs is that now we get a large percentage of the handle [the total money bet] that way—47 percent of all racing, and 6 percent of live racing. It also varies by the day of the meet. We get 64 percent of the handle through VLTs on Tuesday, and only 13 percent on Saturday when the machines are busier. With vouchers, we know that 66 to 70 percent of race winnings are re-bet on the VLTs. Still, racing is only 1 to 6 percent of the gaming handle."

The experiment still doesn't necessarily prove anything. A horse bettor could use the VLT to make his bet, yet never make a slots bet.

My fear about all this is that, with the tail wagging the dog, and with income at tracks breaking down 80 percent slots and 20 percent horses, future managers will tend to spend less and less on racing and more and more on turning the whole facility into a slots parlor. Then all you have is a casino that happens to have horses running around out back. If the idea of this is to strengthen horse racing, wouldn't it be better to put *all* the profit into better purses, which leads to better horses, which leads to better races, which leads to excitement based on the sport itself?

But even if you did that, eventually the slots player would start screaming that he's being neglected. There's already some grumbling that the comp system favors the horseplayer over the slots bettor, which is pretty much true. And the slots player is going to be bored with any details about why you need bigger purses and better horses.

As Ray Bailiff of the Oklahoma Racing Commission put it, "All he knows is that twenty minutes is a long time to wait to be entertained for two minutes."

Periodical Bibliography

The following articles have been selected to supplement the diverse views presented in this chapter.

Rich Archer | "Video Lottery Terminals Reinvigorate Upstate Raceway: Yonkers Eyes Similar Operations," *Westchester County* (New York) *Business Journal*, August 30, 2004.

James Burton | "The Machines That Ate My Life," *New Statesman*, February 21, 2005.

Kim Clark | "Against the Odds," *U.S. News & World Report*, May 23, 2005.

Joseph A. Corbo Jr. | "Meadowlands Slots Would Hurt Casinos," *Newark* (NJ) *Star-Ledger*, August 20, 2006.

Justin Ellis | "Slot Machines Save Day at Dover Downs in Delaware," *Portland* (ME) *Press Herald*, October 5, 2003.

Bill Finley | "Slots Becoming an Expensive Proposition for Tracks," ESPN.com, February 13, 2003. www.espn.com.

Sarah McQuillen | "Maritime Churches Say 'No Dice' to VLTs," *United Church Observer*, July/August 2005.

Shawna Richer | "Staggering Losses," *Globe & Mail* (Toronto), June 24, 2005.

Gary Rivlin | "The Chrome-Shiny, Lights-Flashing, Wheel-Spinning, Touch-Screened, Drew-Carey-Wisecracking, Video-Playing, 'Sound Events' Packed, Pulse-Quickening Bandit," *New York Times Magazine*, May 9, 2004.

Tom Rogers | "Rely on Racinos?" *American Quarter Horse Racing Journal*, November 2005.

Amy Whitfield | "Weil: Racino Model Isn't Industry's Savior," BloodHorse.com, December 6, 2005. www.bloodhorse.com.

For Further Discussion

Chapter 1

1. Frank J. Fahrenkopf Jr. maintains that casino gambling can aid communities by increasing tourism, providing jobs, and generating tax revenue. For Faith & Family contends that the supposed economic benefits of casinos do not outweigh their detrimental social impact—increasing crime in their communities and ruining the lives and finances of problem gamblers and their families. Which argument do you believe is stronger? Why?

2. Native American reservations have traditionally been some of the most economically depressed regions of the nation. The members of the Washington tribes mentioned in Dave Palermo's viewpoint argue that gambling has been a way to create jobs and fund health care and other services so desperately needed on reservations. The Navajo spokespeople in Candi Cushman's viewpoint, however, suggest that the promise of tribal gambling may enrich a few but may also increase problems—such as alcoholism and domestic disputes—for a people already crippled by these social ills. Do you think gaming is a way for Native Americans to improve their communities, or are there reasons that hosting casinos may not be beneficial for all tribes? Explain your answer using the viewpoints in the chapter as well as any other information you can find on experiments in tribal gaming.

Chapter 2

1. After reading all of the viewpoints in Chapter 2, reconsider the supposed negative social effects of Internet gambling. Do you think these possible harms justify a ban on Internet gambling? Explain. In contemplating your answer,

consider whether it would be hypocritical to ban Internet gambling but let other forms of gambling exist legally. Use examples from the viewpoints to strengthen your final argument.

2. Many of those who oppose a ban on Internet gambling argue that it is unconstitutional and not the government's job to police what adults do with their time and money. Those who support a ban often cite as reasons the ease with which children might access Internet gaming sites and the possible harms that Internet gaming might exacerbate in problem gamblers. Do you believe that the American government has a duty to protect its citizens from such potentially harmful behaviors, or is a ban an infringement of individual rights? Use quotes from the viewpoints to support your statements.

Chapter 3

1. After reading the viewpoints in this chapter, do you believe that pathological gambling is a problem best solved by individuals taking responsibility for their actions, or is it a social problem that needs to be addressed by communities—or the nation—as a whole? Explain your reasoning and support it with quotes from the viewpoints.

2. After examining the stories in the two viewpoints on casinos and compulsive gambling, decide whether you think casinos are doing enough to respond to problem gambling. Is it possible that casinos would try to profit from problem gamblers, or is it more likely that casinos would view problem gamblers as risky players who might not be able to pay their debts? Use information from the viewpoints by Steve Friess and Liz Benston to support your answer.

Chapter 4

1. Sol Boxenbaum argues that video lottery terminals (VLTs) are the most addictive form of legalized gambling and

therefore access to the machines must be limited. Fox Butterfield argues for the importance of VLT revenue for different states with limited income resources. After reading both arguments, do you think that the costs of operating VLTs outweigh the benefits for states? Use examples from the viewpoints to support your answer.

2. Joe Bob Briggs argues that the new trend of adding casino gaming to racetracks is wrongheaded and will hurt the integrity of horse racing. In his view, casino gamblers have no interest in racing, and horse race fans are equally uninterested in casino games. Greg Melikov, however, contends that without the infusion of casino money, the horse racing industry would fold because its clientele has been declining for years. Do you think the racino craze is the salvation for horse racing, or might there be another solution to bolster attendance at racetracks? Or, do you believe that the racing industry is not worth saving? Explain your view.

Organizations to Contact

The editors have compiled the following list of organizations concerned with the issues debated in this book. The descriptions are derived from materials provided by the organizations. All have publications or information available for interested readers. The list was compiled on the date of publication of the present volume; the information provided here may change. Be aware that many organizations take several weeks or longer to respond to inquiries, so allow as much time as possible.

American Gaming Association (AGA)
1299 Pennsylvania Ave. NW, Suite 1175
Washington, DC 20004
(202) 552-2675 • fax: (202) 552-2676
e-mail: info@americangaming.org
Web site: www.americangaming.org

The American Gaming Association represents the commercial casino entertainment industry. It informs the general public, elected officials, and other decision makers about the gaming industry. It also lobbies for and against federal legislation affecting tourism, gambling regulations, and other gaming matters. AGA publishes industry newsletters, and its Web site archives many speeches and studies that extol what the organization perceives are the virtues of legalized gambling in America.

Cato Institute
1000 Massachusetts Ave. NW, Washington, DC 20001-5403
(202) 842-0200 • fax: (202) 842-3490
Web site: www.cato.org

The Cato Institute is a libertarian public-policy research foundation. It evaluates government policies and offers reform proposals and commentary both in print and on its Web site. Its publications (collected on its Web site) include the Cato

Policy Analysis series of reports, which have included *Gambling in America: Balancing the Risks of Gambling and Its Regulation* and *Internet Gambling: Popular, Inexorable, and (Eventually) Legal.* It also publishes the magazines *Regulation* and the *Cato Policy Report.*

Focus on the Family
8605 Explorer Dr., Colorado Springs, CO   80995
(800) 232-6459
Web site: www.family.org

Focus on the Family is a nonprofit Christian ministry working to help preserve traditional values and the institution of the family. Its message is carried through *Focus on the Family* magazine and in radio broadcasts. The organization is opposed to all forms of gambling because of its supposed negative impact on families. The Focus on the Family Web site houses many ministry fact sheets on the harms associated with gambling. Other resources such as books, videotapes, and audiotapes on gambling are available on the site for a donation fee.

Gamblers Anonymous (GA)
PO Box 17173, Los Angeles, CA   90017
(213) 386-8789 • fax: (213) 386-0030
e-mail: isomain@gamblersanonymous.org
Web site: www.gamblersanonymous.org

Gamblers Anonymous is a fellowship of men and women who share with each other a commitment to overcome their gambling problems and to help others do the same. Gamblers Anonymous is only a support group, and therefore it neither endorses nor opposes gambling regulation. The organization has branches in all fifty states and in many foreign nations. On its Web site, GA provides a list of twenty questions that gamblers can use to evaluate whether their own gambling has become problematic or compulsive. The site also includes the twelve-step program that members use to combat their desire to gamble.

Institute for Research on Pathological Gambling and Related Disorders
Harvard Medical School, Medford, MA 02155
(781) 306-8604
Web site: www.divisiononaddictions.org/institute

Opened in 2000 as a branch of the Division on Addiction at Harvard Medical School, the Institute for Research on Pathological Gambling conducts and publishes research on the impact of problem gambling on individuals and society. The institute publishes the free weekly online research journal the *WAGER (Weekly Addiction Gambling Education Report)*, which charts studies and new information on problem gambling.

Institute for the Study of Gambling and Commercial Gaming
College of Business Administration, University of Nevada
Reno, NV 89557-0208
(775) 784-1442 • fax: (775) 784-1057
Web site: www.unr.edu/gaming

The institute offers courses and degrees in casino management and other aspects of the gaming industry. It holds national and international conferences on gambling and publishes proceedings from them. The institute produces quarterly reports on current issues and trends in the industry. It also copublishes, with the National Council on Problem Gambling, the quarterly *Journal of Gambling Studies*.

Interactive Gaming Council (IGC)
175-2906 W. Broadway, Vancouver, BC V6K 2G8
   Canada
(604) 732-3833 • fax: (604) 732-3866
e-mail: info@igcouncil.org
Web site: www.igcouncil.org

The Interactive Gaming Council is a nonprofit organization that provides a forum to discuss all aspects of Internet gaming. The organization was originally formed in the United

States, but government opposition to Internet gambling compelled the IGC to relocate to Canada. The IGC continues to urge the U.S. government to repeal its ban on Internet gaming and work toward a means to regulate the new industry. The IGC Web site archives news items and testimonies on Internet gaming.

Jockey Club
40 E. Fifty-second St., New York, NY   10022
(212) 371-5970 • fax: (212) 371-6123
Web site: www.jockeyclub.com

The Jockey Club was formed in 1894 to oversee the breeding and racing of thoroughbred horses in America. Since its inception, the club has kept a registry of all thoroughbred horses in North America. Through its own rule book, the club and its member associations across the country strive to maintain standards in thoroughbred racing. The Jockey Club Web site lists its member organizations and provides some information on thoroughbred racing and breeding. The site also houses an electronic copy of the Jockey Club rule book.

National Center for Responsible Gaming (NCRG)
PO Box 14323, Washington, DC   20044-4323
(202) 552-2689
e-mail: contact@ncrg.org
Web site: www.ncrg.org

The National Center for Responsible Gaming is an organization devoted to funding scientific research on pathological and youth gambling. NCRG-sponsored researchers improve strategies for the prevention and treatment of problem gambling. The center publishes annual reports, press releases, and member-written publications—many of which are available on its Web site. The NCRG also cosponsors (with the American Gaming Association) *Responsible Gaming Quarterly*, a journal related to problem gambling.

National Coalition Against Legalized Gambling (NCALG)
100 Maryland Ave. NE, Rm. 311, Washington, DC   20002
(800) 664-2680
e-mail: ncalg@ncalg.org
Web site: www.ncalg.org

The National Coalition Against Legalized Gambling is concerned with the rapid expansion of gambling across the United States. It maintains that legalized gambling has negatively affected the family, the government, and society and has promoted the problem of youth gambling. NCALG speaks out against the gaming industry in every forum possible. It also supports other groups seeking to curb the expansion of gaming. The NCALG Web site archives many articles relating to the supposed ills of gambling as well as testimony and press releases by NCALG members.

National Congress of American Indians (NCAI)
1301 Connecticut Ave. NW, Suite 200
Washington, DC   20036
(202) 466-7767 • fax: (202) 466-7797
e-mail: ncai@ncai.org
Web site: www.ncai.org

The National Congress of American Indians represents many Native American tribes and aims to protect Indian rights and sovereignty. The NCAI maintains that gaming is one of these tribal rights, and NCAI members have spoken at many venues in defense of Native American gaming. The NCAI Web site houses a few testimonies given before gaming regulatory commissions and other government bodies.

National Council of Legislators from Gaming States (NCLGS)
385 Jordan Rd., Troy, NY   12180
(518) 687-0615 • fax: (518) 687-0401
e-mail: info@nclgs.org
Web site: www.nclgs.org

The National Council of Legislators from Gaming States is a nonpartisan assembly of state lawmakers (representing forty-four states and the District of Columbia) who meet regularly to discuss issues related to gaming and its regulation. The NCLGS was a sponsor of the Public Sector Gaming Study Commission (PSGSC), an investigative body that examined the economic, social, and political impact of gaming in America. The PSGSC's final report (issued in 2000) and other NCLGS press releases are accessible on the council's Web site.

National Council on Problem Gambling
216 G St. NE, Suite 200, Washington, DC   20002
(202) 547-9204 • fax: (202) 547-9206
e-mail: ncpg@ncpgambling.org
Web site: www.ncpgambling.org

The mission of the National Council on Problem Gambling is to increase public awareness of pathological gambling, increase treatment for problem gamblers and their families, and encourage research and programs for prevention and education. The council publishes informational pamphlets such as "Problem and Pathological Gambling in America" and "When Someone You Love Gambles."

National Indian Gaming Association (NIGA)
224 Second St. SE, Washington, DC   20003
(202) 546-7711 • fax: (202) 546-1755
e-mail: info@indiangaming.org
Web site: www.indiangaming.org

The National Indian Gaming Association is a nonprofit organization of 168 Indian nations that are engaged in tribal gaming. The NIGA's mission is to protect and preserve the general welfare of tribes that are striving for self-sufficiency through gaming enterprises. The association works with the federal government and Congress to develop sound policies and practices and to provide opinions on gaming-related issues. It publishes a newsletter, and the NIGA Web site contains an archive of testimony from tribal leaders on the benefits of Indian gaming, as well as other documents related to the subject.

North American Association of State and Provincial Lotteries (NASPL)
2775 Bishop Rd., Suite B, Willoughby Hills, OH   44092
(216) 241-2310 • fax: (216) 241-4350
e-mail: info@nasplhq.org
Web site: www.naspl.org

The North American Association of State and Provincial Lotteries is a nonprofit organization that represents forty-seven lottery organizations in North America. Its main function is to gather and disseminate information on the perceived benefits of such lotteries. The NASPL Web site contains an overview of lottery history, testimony concerning lottery myths, and a searchable database—the NASPL Resource Link, containing information on the lottery available by subscription.

North American Gaming Regulators Association (NAGRA)
1000 Westgate Dr., Suite 252, St. Paul, MN   55114
(651) 203-7244 • fax: (651) 290-2266
Web site: www.nagra.org

The North American Gaming Regulators Association is composed of members of federal, state, local, provincial, and tribal government agencies that are involved in gaming regulation. NAGRA's mission is to unify the standards and practices of gaming enterprises across North America. The association holds regular meetings and publishes a newsletter that can be downloaded from its Web site.

United Methodist Church General Board of Church and Society
100 Maryland Ave. NE, Washington, DC   20002
(202) 488-5600
Web site: www.umc-gbcs.org

This department of the United Methodist Church believes that "gambling is a menace to society; deadly to the best interests of moral, social, economic, and spiritual life; and destructive of good government." The board urges Christians and others to abstain from gambling, and it opposes state promotion and legalization of gambling. The board's Web site offers (for a fee) an antigambling information packet that includes position papers, pamphlets, and article reprints.

University of Nevada at Las Vegas Libraries
Gaming Collection
4505 Maryland Pkwy., Box 457010
Las Vegas, NV   89154-7010
(702) 895-2242 • fax: (702) 895-2253
e-mail: dgs@unlv.nevada.edu
Web site: www.library.unlv.edu/speccol/gaming

The University of Nevada at Las Vegas (UNLV) library houses the largest collection of resources on the history, regulation, politics, psychology, and statistical bases of gambling. The entire gaming collection can be visited at the UNLV campus, but many documents in the collection can be accessed online. The gaming collection Web site also hosts a virtual museum of artwork and other visual elements relating to gambling.

Bibliography of Books

Herbert Asbury — *Sucker's Progress: An Informal History of Gambling in America from the Colonies to Canfield.* New York: Dodd, Mead, 1938.

Thomas Barker and Marjie Britz — *Jokers Wild: Legalized Gambling in the Twenty-first Century.* Westport, CT: Praeger, 2000.

Jeff Benedict — *Without Reservation: The Making of America's Most Powerful Indian Tribe and the World's Largest Casino.* New York: HarperCollins, 2000.

Mary O. Borg, Paul M. Mason, and Stephen L. Shapiro — *The Economic Consequences of State Lotteries.* New York: Praeger, 1991.

Larry Braidfoot — *Gambling: A Deadly Game.* Nashville: Broadman, 1985.

Tyler Bridges — *Bad Bet on the Bayou: The Rise of Gambling in Louisiana and the Fall of Governor Edwin Edwards.* New York: Farrar, Straus and Giroux, 2002.

Henry Chafetz — *Play the Devil: A History of Gambling in the United States from 1492 to 1955.* New York: Clarkson N. Potter, 1960.

Charles T. Clotfelter and Philip J. Cook — *Selling Hope: State Lotteries in America.* Cambridge, MA: Harvard University Press, 1989.

Peter Collins   *Gambling and the Public Interest.* Westport, CT: Praeger, 2003.

Eve Darian-Smith   *New Capitalists: Law, Politics, and Identity Surrounding Casino Gaming on Native American Land.* Belmont, CA: Wadsworth, 2004.

Richard O. Davies and Richard G. Abram   *Betting the Line: Sports Wagering in American Life.* Columbus: Ohio State University Press, 2001.

Sally Denton and Roger Morris   *The Money and the Power: The Making of Las Vegas and Its Hold on America, 1947–2000.* New York: Knopf, 2001.

John Dombrink and William N. Thompson   *The Last Resort: Success and Failure in Campaigns for Casinos.* Reno: University of Nevada Press, 1990.

William R. Eadington and Judy A. Cornelius, eds.   *Indian Gaming and the Law.* 2nd ed. Reno: University of Nevada Press, 1998.

Kim Isaac Eisler   *Revenge of the Pequots: How a Small Native American Tribe Created the World's Most Profitable Casino.* New York: Simon & Schuster, 2001.

John M. Findlay   *People of Chance: Gambling in American Society from Jamestown to Las Vegas.* New York: Oxford University Press, 1986.

Brett Duval Fromson   *Hitting the Jackpot: The Inside Story of the Richest Indian Tribe in History.* New York: Atlantic Monthly, 2003.

Robert Goodman   *The Luck Business: The Devastating Consequences and Broken Promises of America's Gambling Explosion.* New York: Free Press, 1995.

Earl L. Grinols   *Gambling in America: Costs and Benefits.* New York: Cambridge University Press, 2004.

David M. Haugen   *Legalized Gambling.* New York: Facts on File, 2006.

Denise von Herrman   *The Big Gamble: The Politics of Lottery and Casino Expansion.* Westport, CT: Praeger, 2002.

Cathy H.C. Hsu, ed.   *Legalized Casino Gaming in the United States: The Economic and Social Impact.* Binghamton, NY: Haworth, 1999.

Nelson Johnson   *Boardwalk Empire: The Birth, High Times, and Corruption of Atlantic City.* Medford, NJ: Plexus, 2002.

David Johnston   *Temples of Chance: How America Inc. Bought Out Murder Inc. to Win Control of the Casino Business.* New York: Doubleday, 1992.

W. Dale Mason   *Indian Gaming: Tribal Sovereignty and American Politics.* Norman: University of Oklahoma Press, 2000.

Richard A. McGowan   *Government and the Transformation of the Gaming Industry.* Northampton, MA: Edward Elgar, 2001.

Richard A. McGowan — *State Lotteries and Legalized Gambling: Painless Revenue or Painful Mirage?* Westport, CT: Praeger, 1994.

Angela Mullis and David Kamper, eds. — *Indian Gaming: Who Wins?* Los Angeles: UCLA American Indian Studies Center, 2000.

David Nibert — *Hitting the Lottery Jackpot: State Governments and the Taxing of Dreams.* New York: Monthly Review, 2000.

Timothy L. O'Brien — *Bad Bet: The Inside Story of the Glamour, Glitz, and Danger of America's Gambling Industry.* New York: Times Business, 1998.

Gerda Reith — *The Age of Chance: Gambling in Western Culture.* New York: Routledge, 1999.

I. Nelson Rose and Martin D. Owens Jr. — *Internet Gaming Law.* Larchmont, NY: Mary Ann Liebert, 2005.

David G. Schwartz — *Cutting the Wire: Gambling Prohibition and the Internet.* Reno: University of Nevada Press, 2005.

David G. Schwartz — *Roll the Bones: The History of Gambling.* New York: Gotham, 2006.

Howard J. Shaffer, ed. — *Futures at Stake: Youth, Gambling, and Society.* Reno: University of Nevada Press, 2003.

David J. Valley and Diana Lindsay — *Jackpot Trail: Indian Gaming in Southern California.* San Diego: Sunbelt, 2003.

Rachel A. Volberg   *When the Chips Are Down: Problem*
Gambling in America. New York:
Century Foundation, 2001.

Index

A

Abramoff, Jack, 91

Addiction to gambling. *See* Compulsive Gambling; Gamblers Anonymous

AGA (American Gaming Association), 15, 20, 33, 153, 167

Age verification for gambling, 112

Albuquerque (NM), 58

Alcoholics Anonymous, 102

Alcoholism, 57–58, 96, 109

Alden, Mark, 110

American Demographics (magazine), 67, 68

American Gaming Association (AGA), 15, 20, 33, 153, 167

American history and gambling, 114

American Insurance Institute, 99

American Prospect (magazine), 146

American Psychiatric Association (APA), 98–103, 131

Analysis Group Inc., 50

Annenberg Public Policy Center, 113

Anti-gambling legislation, 29

Anti-gambling organizations, 107–108, 168, 169, 171, 172

Antigua, 92

APA (American Psychiatric Association), 98–103, 131

Arizona, 56

Associated Press, 60

Association of Problem Gambling Service Administrators, 107–108

Atlantic City (NJ) casinos, 16, 123

B

Bachus, Spencer, 67

Bailiff, Ray, 162

Balko, Radley, 85

Bankruptcies and gambling, 32, 43–44

Banning Internet gambling. *See* Internet gambling, banning

Barbour, Haley, 14

Bartlett, Donald L., 59

Baxandall, Phineas, 37, 42

BBC (British Broadcasting Corporation), 110

Benefits of gambling. *See* Society, benefiting of gambling to

Bennett, William, 105

Benston, Liz, 127

BetOnSports (Internet gambling corporation), 66, 80, 82

Betting on sports, 65–66, 69, 70, 91–92

Biblical principles and gambling, 23–24

Bingo, 15, 105

Boldt, George, 53

Bortolin, Greg, 125

Boxenbaum, Sol, 137

Brain disorders, 98–103

Briggs, Joe Bob, 156

British Broadcasting Corporation (BBC), 110

Broward County (FL), 125, 151, 152

Brown, Bryan, 154

Buffalo Research Institute on Addictions, 57

Bureau of Indian Affairs, 49